# ENTER THE DRAGON

## Photo Collection
## Volume Two

"Enter the Dragon Photo Collection Volume Two", by Rick Baker
Edited by Rick Baker. Foreword by Rick Baker
Photographs from the EH Archives

Special thanks to: K.Reeve, George Tan, Ting Wai Ho, Nic Cairns, Nick Singh, Alan Donkin. And a special mention to Gary Burton who got me my first ticket to see this movie, after five failed attempts for being under-age.
Special mention to my mum who was as big a kung fu movie fans as me.
Special thanks to Steve K for maintaining my love of Bruce Lee.
Special thanks to Sylvester (Sly) Raymond for being a good friend.

Special dedication to Chan Yuk. Thank you for the many images and moments in time you left, of one of the greatest icons the world has even known – BRUCE LEE, 1940 – 1973

Every effort to trace the copyright holders of the illustrations and original layouts in this book. In the event that any have been inadvertently overlooked, please contact the publishers so that the situation can be rectified in future editions.

Please note: The photographs within these pages have been presented in their best quality format. Some original negatives had slight damage and it was decided to leave them as seen for authenticity (sometimes over exposed and slighty out of focus). Some contact sheets had light scratches due to age. Printing on a matt paper can sometimes highlight these issues, but time and care has been taken with the images used to give the reader the best quality presentation.

First published by Eastern Heroes 2020
www.easternheroes.com
FIRST EDITION

Printed by © Copyright 2020 Ingram Content Group, www.ingramspark.com. All Rights Reserved.
Design & Layout, Nic Cairns, 22:22 Creative Media

ISBN: 978-1-8380706-4-9

All rights reserved. No parts of this publication may be reproduced or transmitted in any form or by any means, graphic, electronic or mechanical, including photocopying, recording, taping or any information storage and retrieval system, without prior written permission of the publisher.

# INTRODUCTION

**E**nter the Dragon **is, without doubt,** the most important and influential martial arts movie ever made. It is a film that inspired and influenced audiences around the globe, and introduced a new icon and superstar to the world – Bruce Lee.

"In the beginning the world had only flirted with martial art movies. It was not until Bruce Lee came along that the world fell in love with them."

# EDIT THE DRAGON

**W**elcome to Volume Two, which presents another showcase of eye-opening photographs from the most iconic martial arts movie ever committed to celluloid.

If you lived in England, it was going to be a while before fans managed to see the complete uncut version of *Enter the Dragon*, due to the BBFC (British Board of Film Censorship) and their 'happy clappy' scissor work. They massacred this seminal movie, which was not presented as Bruce intended.

This was immensely frustrating, as we Brits were soon to become aware that we had been short-changed. It was an absurd situation, and revealed the dichotomy between overbearing censorship and real life. Even though we were not getting the complete movie, we could see photos in the various magazines that flooded the market after its release, fully depicting the cut scenes. Scenes that were as brutally removed as the violence they depicted!

We still had the nunchakus scene though, right? Not for long. Enter stage right, Mr James Ferman. Despite not being involved in the cuts to the 1973 cinema release, in 1979 he recalled the movie from circulation. His primary target of interest was the scene depicting Bruce using the nunchakus, a weapon that had been obscure to the Western world until Bruce Lee had gained infamy for demonstrating their use in *Enter the Dragon*.

It was a weapon that Bruce Lee used with such ease, that most who tried to imitate him ended up doing more damage to themselves than anyone else. Nevertheless, more and more people were either buying or making their own crude versions, with broomstick handles cut down and linked by a piece of chain. James Ferman took issue with this.

Years later, I remember going into the BBFC when my company was submitting movies for classification and asking about the scenes cut by James Ferman in 1979. Apparently out of all the films he had censored, *Enter the Dragon* had received the most complaints. I was told that there was a folder in his office packed with letters, highlighting the issue of attacks by thugs wielding home-made nunchakus, mainly on the football terraces and in random gang exchanges.

It was stated to me that *Enter the Dragon* had unwittingly primed the British film industry for a period of aggressive censorship; it was a catalyst for a stricter era of interventions. The nunchakus had inspired real-life violence and assaults, as noted by police after the film's release in Britain.

This rise in violence coincided with James Ferman becoming well established in his role at the BBFC. A perfect storm – it seemed that James Ferman hated nunchakus! As such, when taking advice from the police to remove the scene entirely, he dutifully obliged.

Ferman wasn't finished there. He also insisted on further measures to have any sign of the iconic weapon removed from the cinema poster, replacing them with a solid stick. The same treatment was applied to the *Way of the Dragon* poster.

However, like all censored films and video nasties, what *Enter the Dragon* lost in the cuts, it gained in notoriety. Despite the changes, a whole generation of British kids had already seen Bruce prominently use the nunchakus in its first release, which raised the argument that Ferman had "closed the stable door after the horse had bolted." He had actually made the film more desirable for people searching for uncut bootleg copies from overseas.

Thankfully, younger people don't have to suffer the censorship that some of us older fans suffered and endured in the '70s and '80s. The BBFC is far more lenient, and we can now see most films uncut, with the exception of certain scenes.

As a reminder, however, here is the chronology of the evolution of *Enter the Dragon* at the hands of the censors:

# From Cut to Complete – Enter the Dragon: A UK Censorship Story.

**1973** – The film was passed with an 'X' certificate by the BBFC, with cuts for the cinematic release. In total there were five cuts made to scenes of violence, including the removal of the broken bottle attack at the end of the Lee/O'Harra fight. But, crucially, the nunchaku scene was left intact.

**1979** – The film was recalled so that a sequence in which Bruce Lee uses his nunchakus to fend off the guards could be deleted, following a surge in real-life hooligan violence, mainly by thugs and football fans attending matches. Also, another sequence in which the nunchakus were seen being carried was cut from the movie.

**1988** – The video version was passed with an '18' certificate, with 1 minute and 45 seconds cut. Three of the five cuts for violence made in 1973 were waived, but two were retained. The first cut was an off-screen neck break. This version cuts away just as Bolo crouches to jerk and snap one of the guard's spines. The second cut occurs when Bolo cradles the final opponent, in order to slowly break his back. The sound effect accompanying this act was shortened.

**1991** – The cuts to the nunchakus scenes implemented in 1979 were retained for the video release. However, the Board modified its policy so that the weapon was no longer removed from sight.

**1991** – A number of representations for the nunchaku scenes were passed, but only when they were not actually in use. The video of *Enter the Dragon* was resubmitted again in 1993 for widescreen release. This time the two remaining cuts for violence were waived, as was the brief sight of nunchakus being carried, in accordance with the new policy. The only cut kept this time was the sight of Bruce Lee twirling and briefly using the nunchakus (21 seconds cut).

**2001** – *Enter the Dragon* was resubmitted in its uncut form and, in accordance with the BBFC's revised policy, was passed as an '18' without cuts.

So, it only took 28 years before the British audience could watch *Enter the Dragon* in its complete form, and I am happy to say that the film's popularity is just as strong today as it was back in 1973. The movie has enjoyed multiple releases and, as I type, has just had another limited edition version released through a high-street media entertainment outlet. These updated releases feature high-grade re-mastering, so the experience of the viewers is upgraded, and we can see those previously-elusive cuts in all their heavenly glory.

*Rick Baker*

# THE CAST

1. Bruce Lee – Lee

2. Shih Kien – Han

3. Sammo Hung – Shaolin Fighter

4. Roy Chiao – Shaolin Abbot

*Enter the Dragon* Photographic Collection – Vol. 2

5. Jim Kelly – Williams

6. John Saxon – Roper

7. Bob Wall – O'Harra

8. Ahna Capri – Tanya

9. Betty Chung – Mey Ling

10. Geoffrey Weeks – Braithwaite

11. Angela Mao Ying – Soo Lin

12. Lam Ching-Ying – Extra

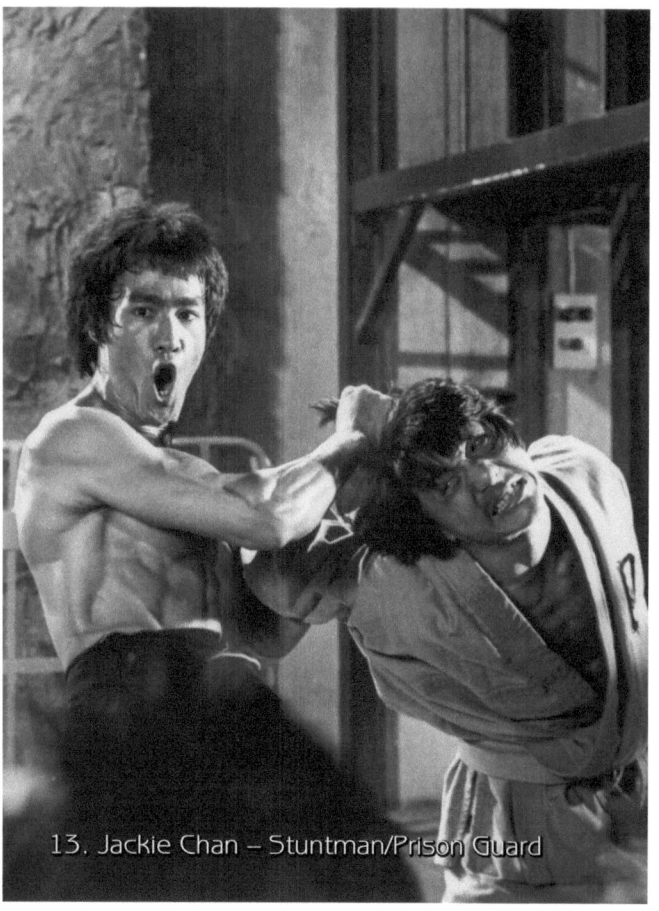

13. Jackie Chan – Stuntman/Prison Guard

14. Yuen Wah – Bruce Lee Double/Stuntman

| | |
|---|---|
| **1) Bruce Lee** | Nothing to add here except without his presence in the lead role, *Enter the Dragon* would not be the masterpiece it is today, becoming a major influence amongst those that saw it upon its release. |
| **2) Shih Kien** | Born on January 1, 1913 in Shigang Village, Panyu, Guangdong, China as Wing-Cheung Shek. He is known for his work on many movies but found popularity playing Han in *Enter the Dragon* (1973). Sadly passed June the 3rd 2009. |
| **3) Sammo Hung** | Born January 7th 1952 in Hong Kong. A very young Sammo played a Shaolin fighter giving him the opportunity to face off with Bruce in the opening scene. He has become an iconic figure amongst kung fu movie fans with his fight choreography and starring roles in many classic movies, too many to mention. |
| **4) Roy Chiao** | Born on March 16, 1927 in Shanghai, China. He played the Shaolin monk who offers Bruce some words of wisdom before Lee embarks on his perilous mission. Roy passed away April 14th 1999. |
| **5) Jim Kelly** | Born May 5, 1946 in Paris, Kentucky, USA. Jim Broke down the colour barrier to become the first black martial artist to become a movie star, playing Williams. Sadly passed away June 29th 2013. |
| **6) John Saxon** | Born August 5th 1936. A black belt in karate, he played Roper, almost losing out to Rod Taylor who was deemed too tall for the role. Sadly passed away this year July 25th 2020. |
| **7) Bob Wall** | Born August 22nd 1939. A close friend of Bruce, he would play Han's bodyguard O'Harra. |
| **8) Ahna Capri** | Born July 6th in Budapest, Hungary. Played the enticing Tania whose charms got the better of Roper. Sadly passed away August 19th 2010. |
| **9) Betty Chung** | Born in 1947, she plays Mei Ling, an undercover operative who has sneaked into Han's compound in search of evidence. |
| **10) Geoffrey Weeks** | Born 1922. Plays Braithwaite, who signs Bruce up for his mission to Han's island. Sadly Geoffrey passed away the following year in 1974. |
| **11) Angela Mao Ying** | Born 20th September 1950 in Taiwan and plays Su Lin, Bruce Lee's sister, who commits suicide rather than fall foul to O'Harra's men. Angela appeared in countless films after being discovered by Raymond Chow. |
| **12) Lam Chin-Ying** | Born 27th December 1952 (Honourable Mention). Played one of Han's lackeys in several scenes but was known as personal assistant to Bruce Lee on Lee's movies including *The Big Boss*, *Fist of Fury*, *Enter the Dragon*, *Way of the Dragon*, and *Game of Death*. Sadly passed away 8th November 1997. |
| **13) Jackie Chan** | Born 7th April 1954 (Honourable Mention). Made several appearances as a prison guard, famously getting killed as Bruce stares into the camera. Little did anyone know he would one day become as famous an icon as Bruce Lee. |
| **14) Yuen Wah** | Born September 2nd 1950 in Hong Kong (Honourable Mention). Plays a prison guard and doubled for Bruce in several scenes, including the somersault after the first fight and the back flip against Bob wall. |

# A ROOM WITHOUT A VIEW

Enter the Dragon Photographic Collection – Vol. 2

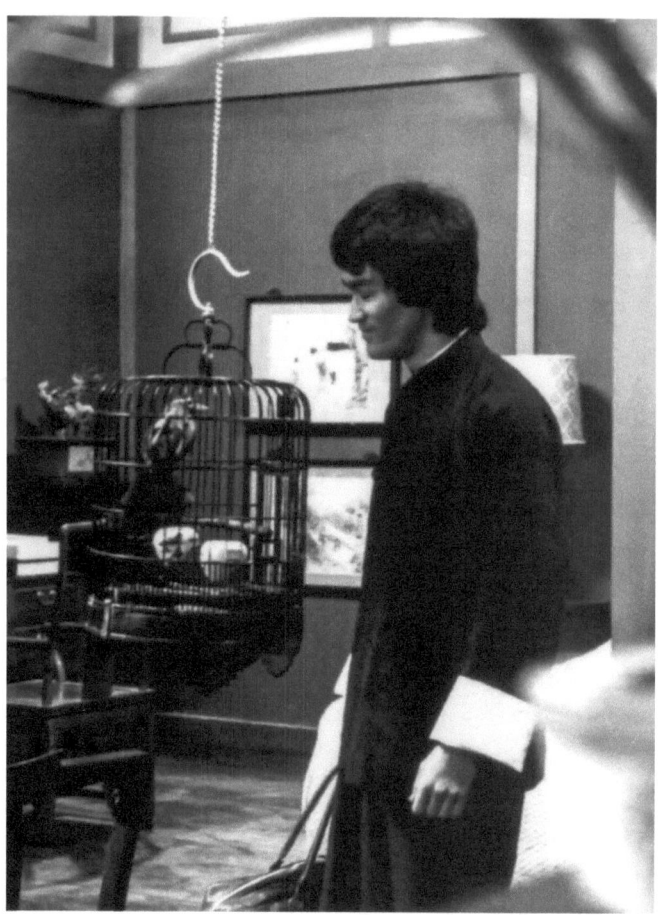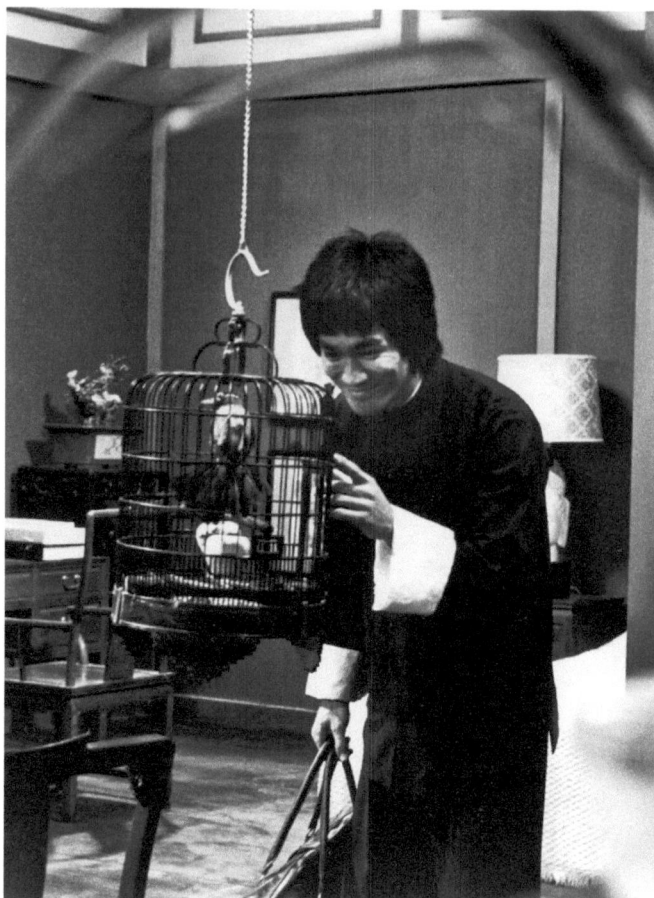

Enter the Dragon Photographic Collection – Vol. 2

# BEHIND THE SCENES

Enter the Dragon Photographic Collection – Vol. 2

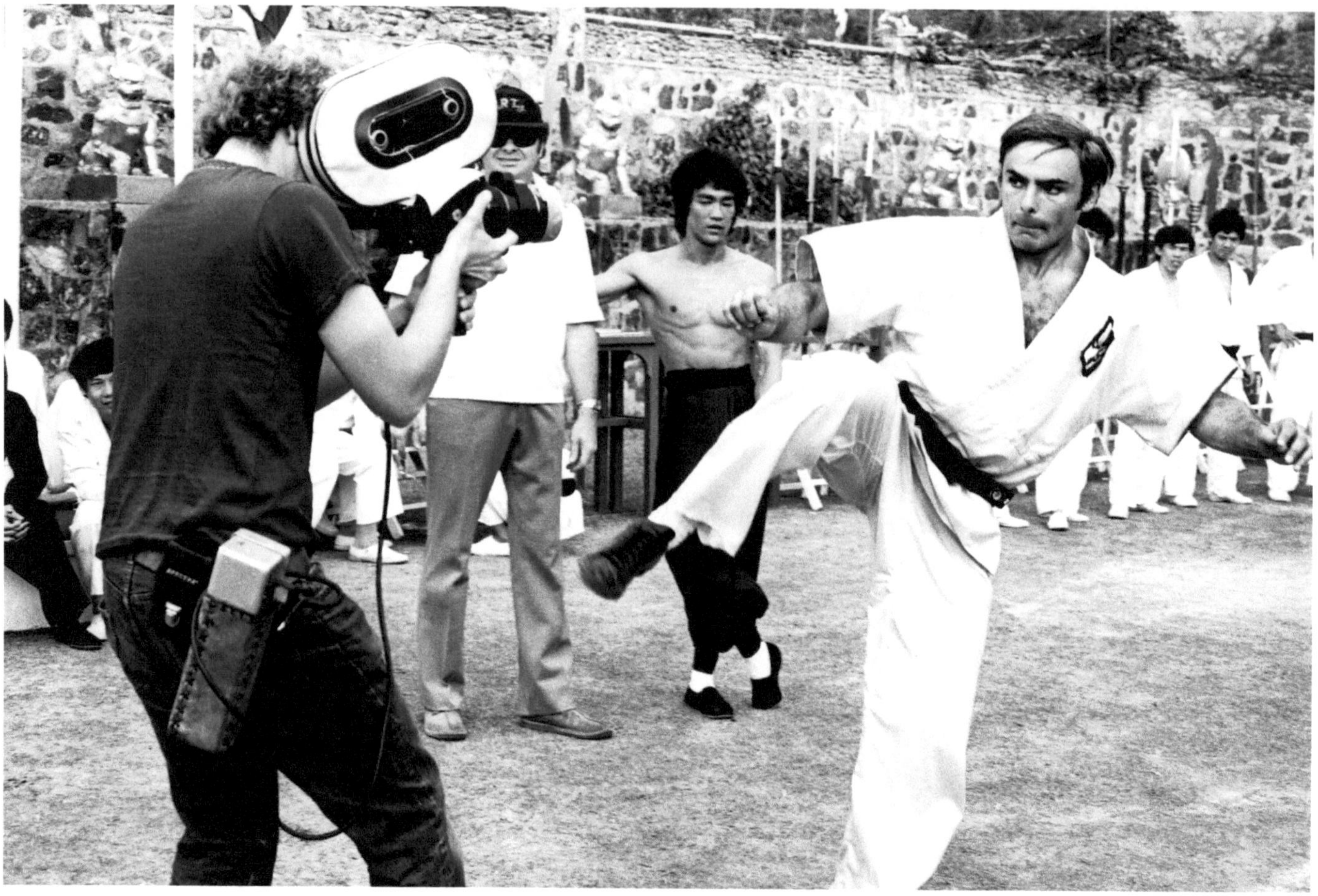

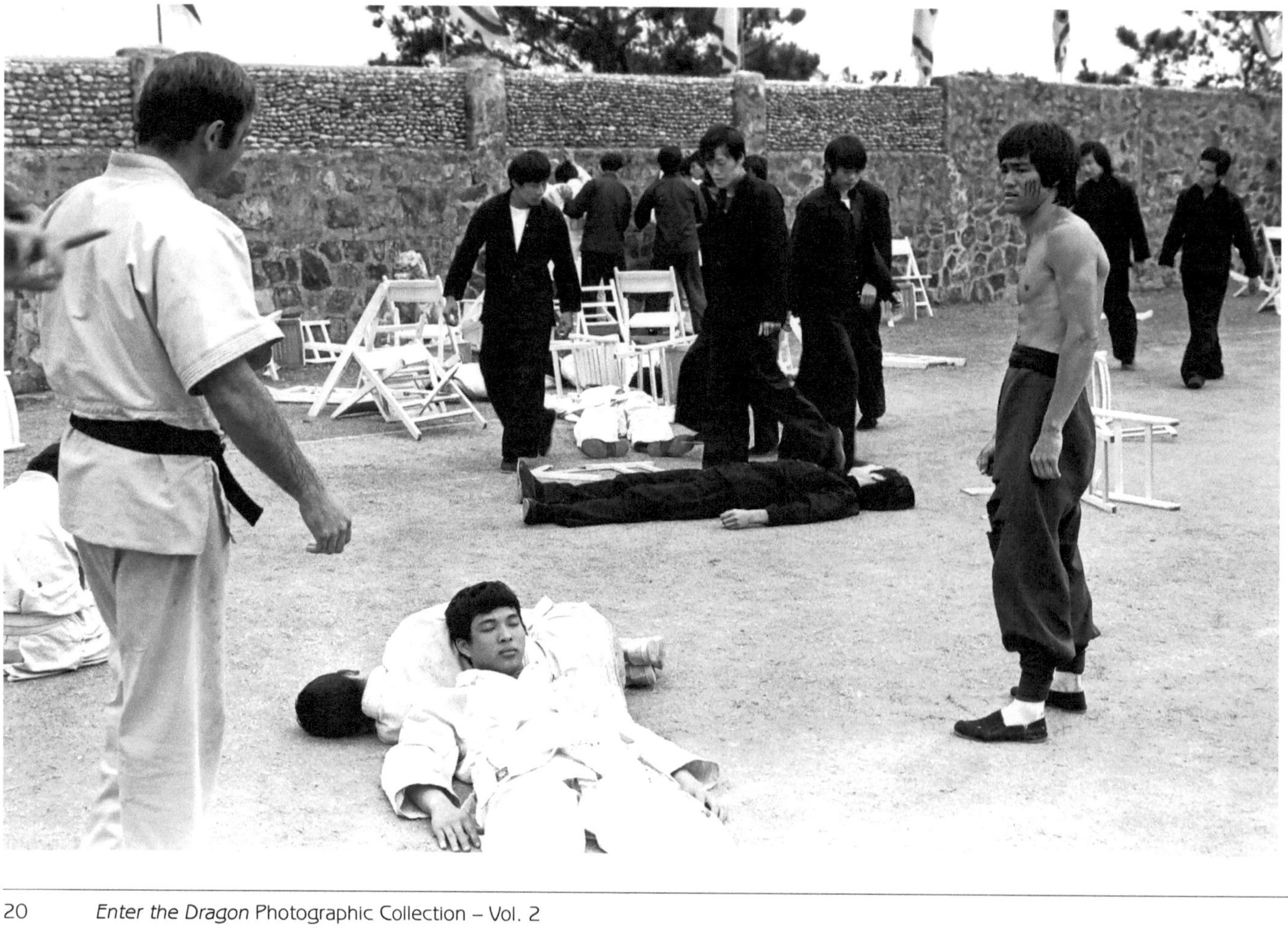

Enter the Dragon Photographic Collection – Vol. 2

22    *Enter the Dragon* Photographic Collection – Vol. 2

*Enter the Dragon* Photographic Collection – Vol. 2

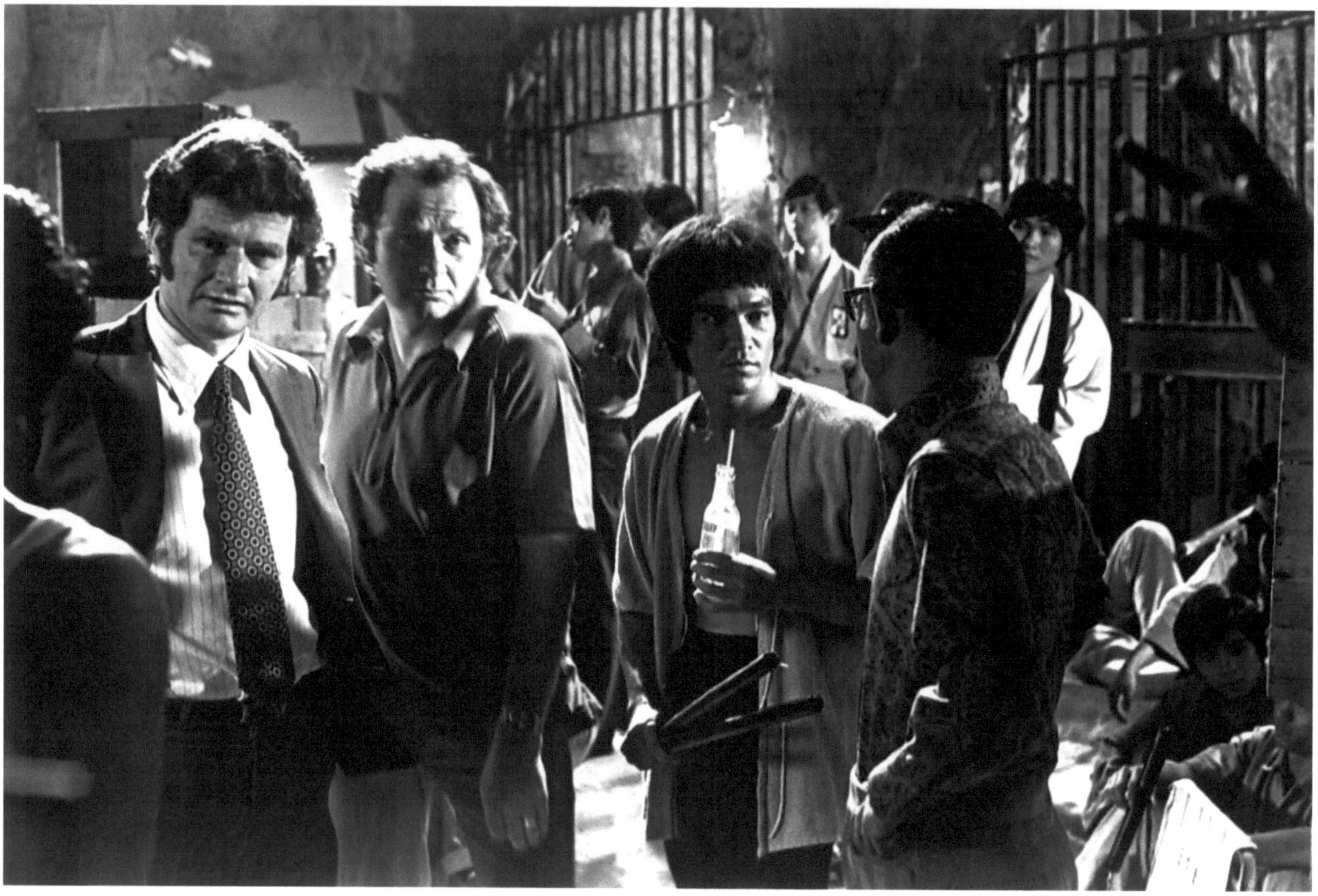

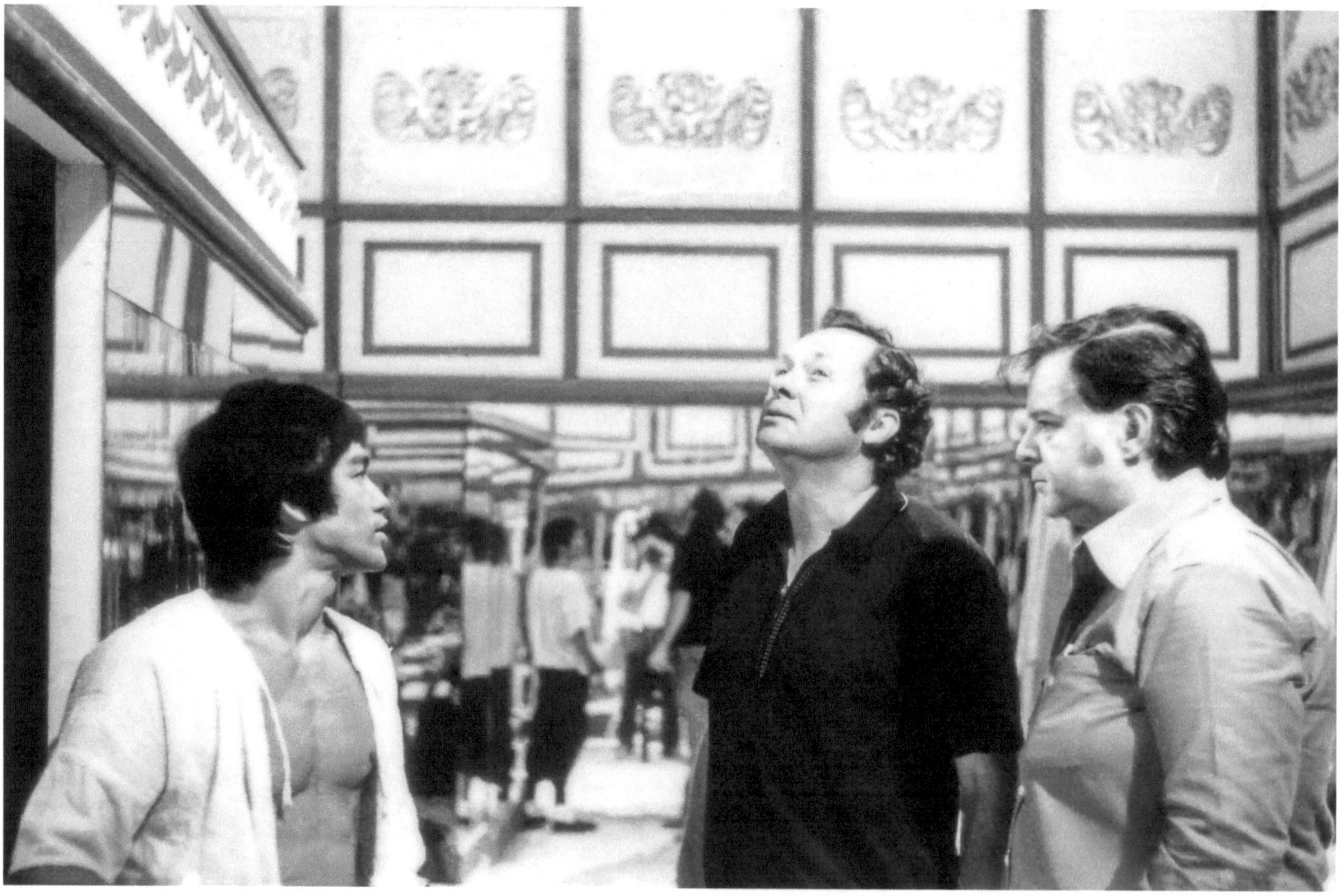

Enter the Dragon Photographic Collection – Vol. 2

# CLASSIC BRUCE LEE POSES

Enter the Dragon Photographic Collection – Vol. 2

# CAPTURING THE ACTION

Enter the Dragon Photographic Collection – Vol. 2

Enter the Dragon Photographic Collection – Vol. 2

38  *Enter the Dragon* Photographic Collection – Vol. 2

44   *Enter the Dragon* Photographic Collection – Vol. 2

**T**he cameraman's shutter speed must have been set to fast as he fired off shots attempting to capture the lightning speed displayed during the fight sequences.

46  *Enter the Dragon* Photographic Collection – Vol. 2

*Enter the Dragon* Photographic Collection – Vol. 2

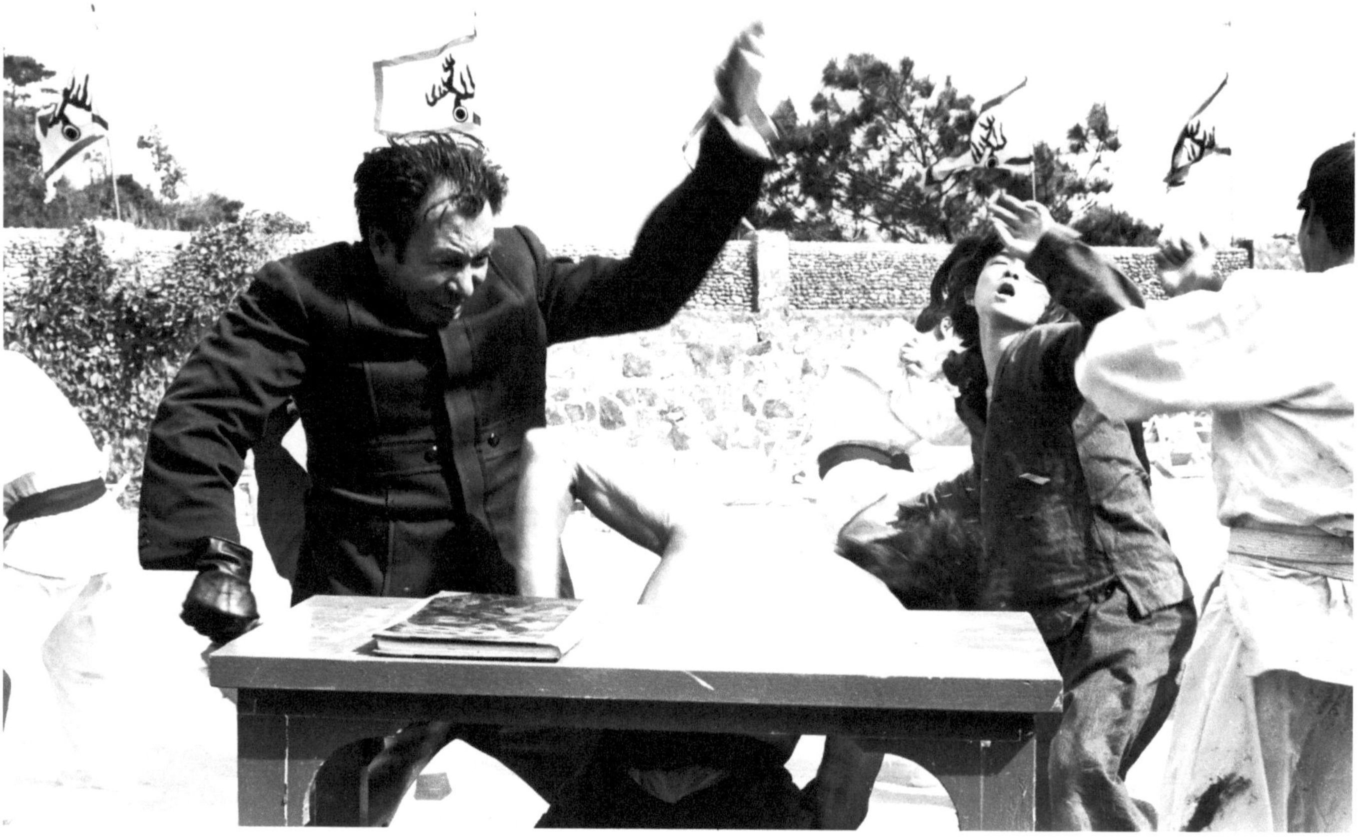

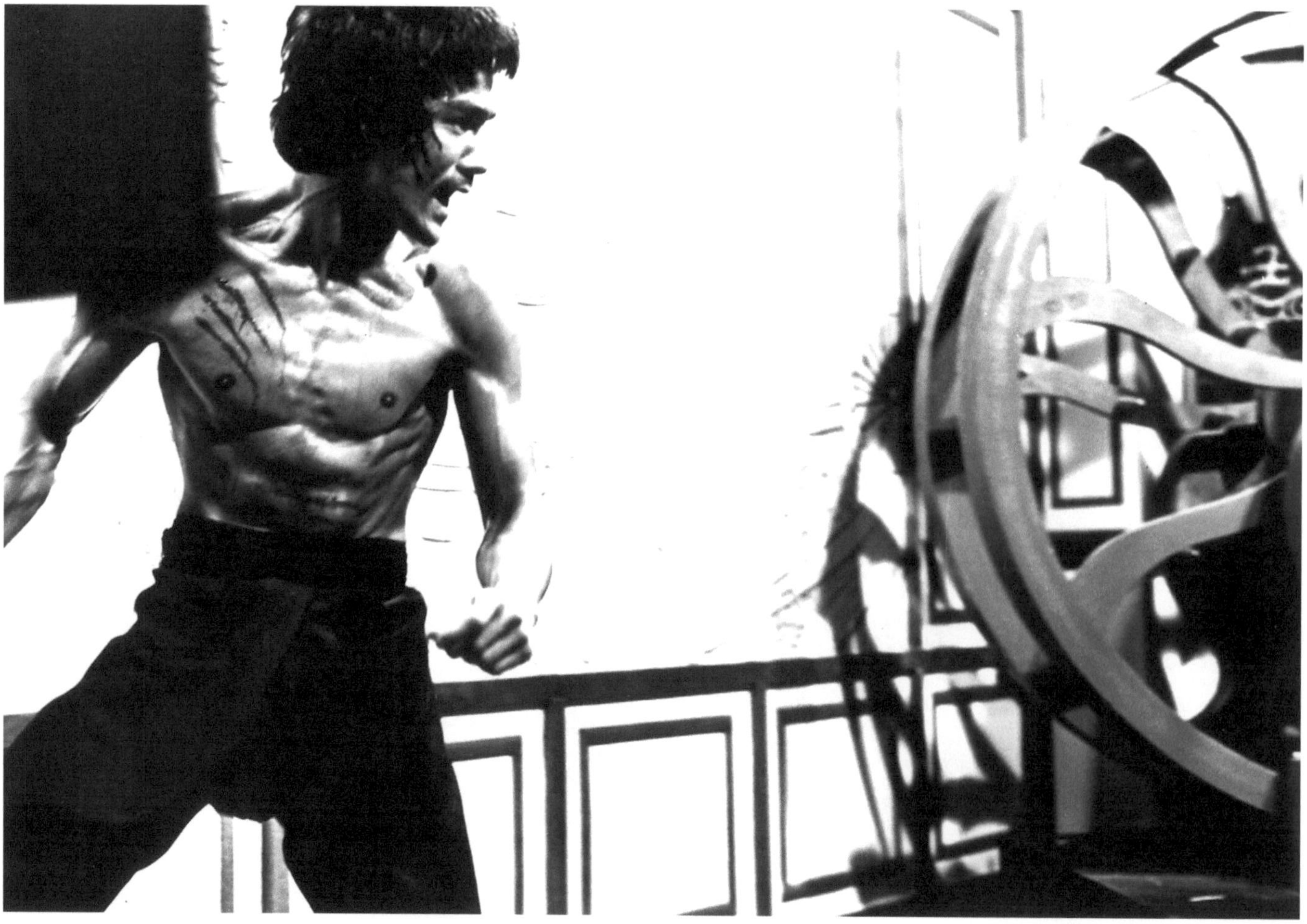

Enter the Dragon Photographic Collection – Vol. 2

# MAN OF A THOUSAND EXPRESSIONS

50  *Enter the Dragon* Photographic Collection – Vol. 2

*Enter the Dragon* Photographic Collection – Vol. 2

**B**ruce Lee's facial expressions were many, from a welcoming smile to moody, to brooding to that of a focused warrior ready to unleash upon all that got in his way.

# PREPPING THE HOUSE OF MIRRORS

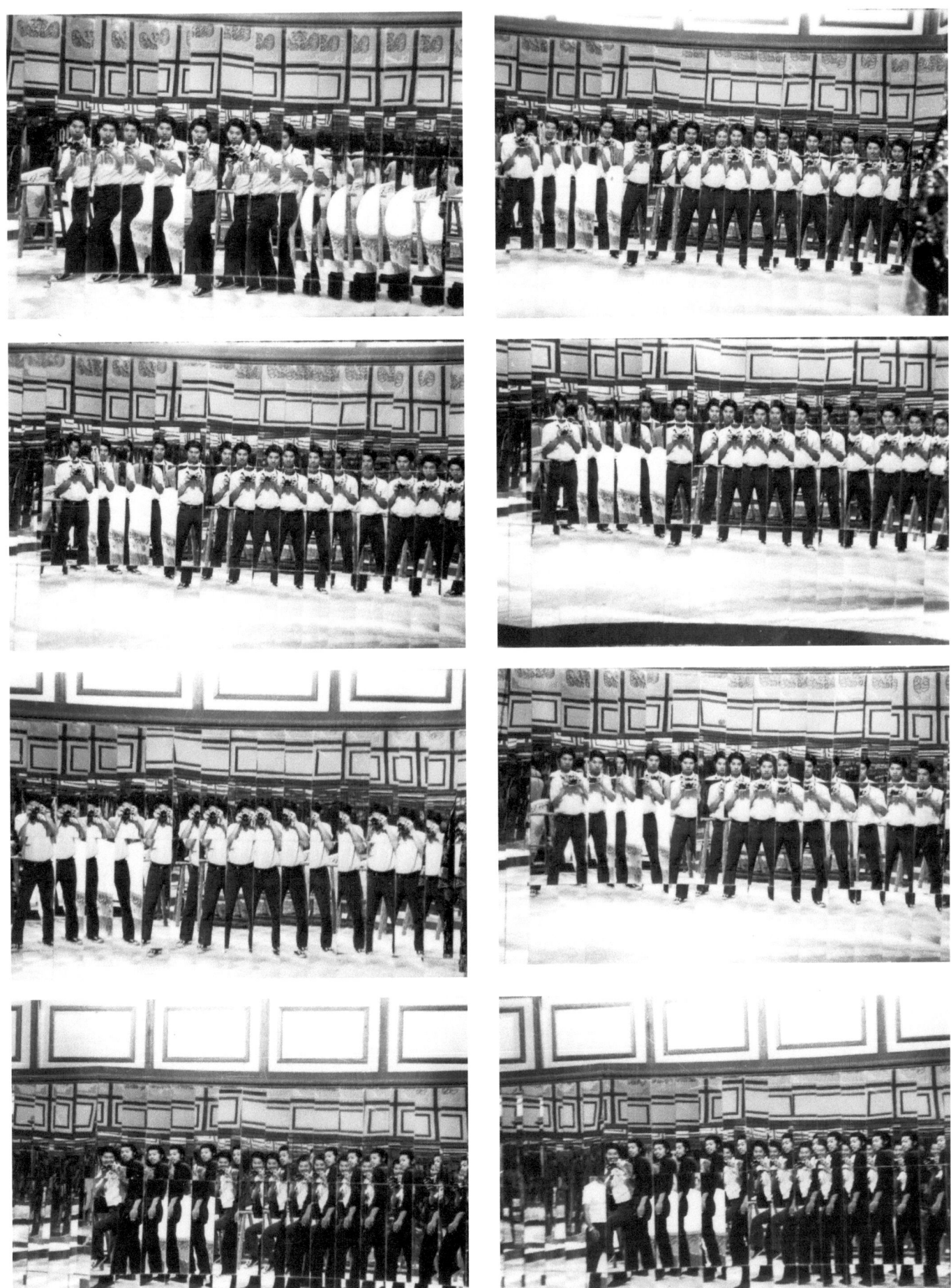

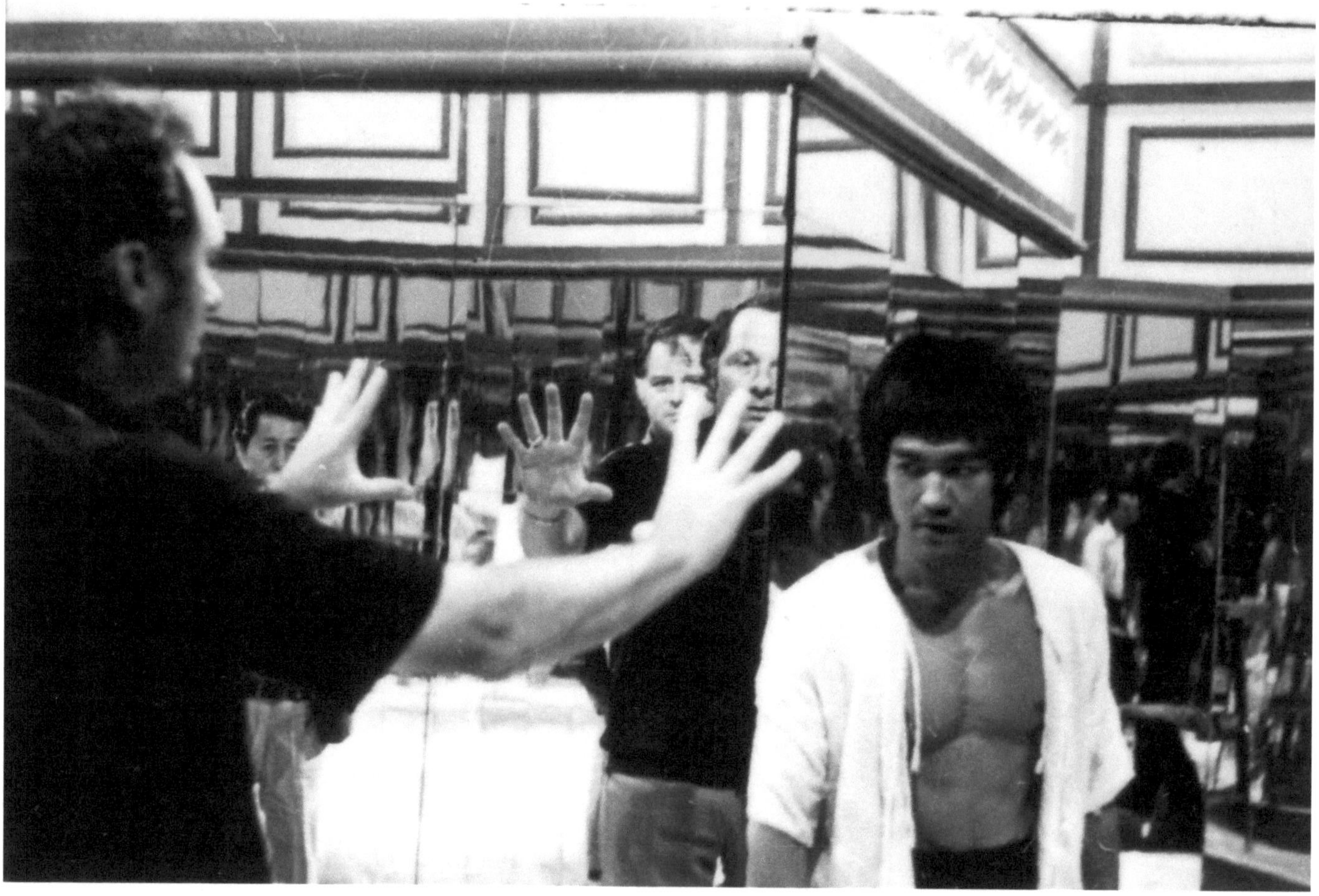

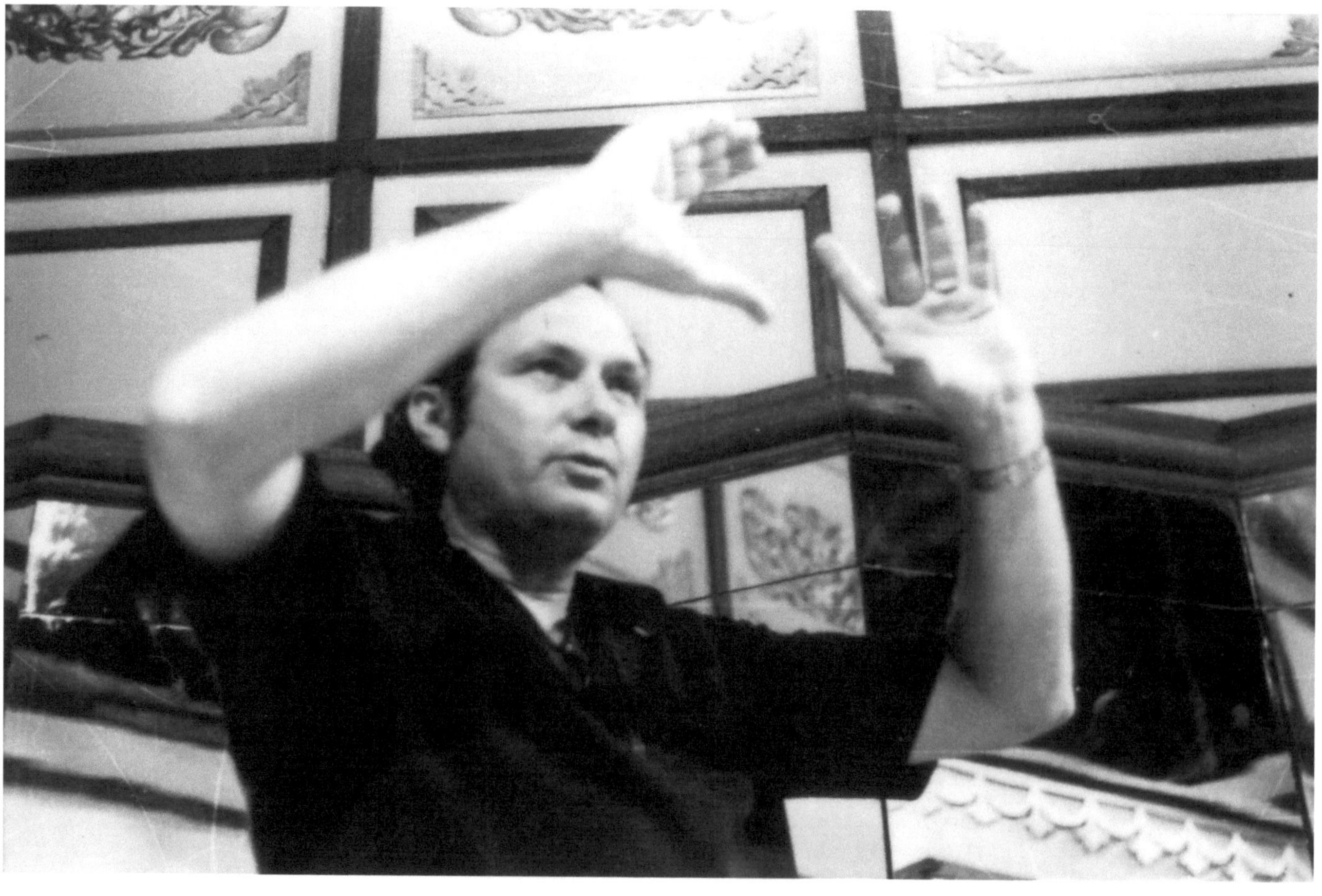

# THE HOUSE OF MIRRORS

Enter the Dragon Photographic Collection – Vol. 2

62   *Enter the Dragon* Photographic Collection – Vol. 2

*Enter the Dragon* Photographic Collection – Vol. 2

# RARE SHOTS FROM CONTACT SHEETS

**T**hese rare pictures are taken from contact sheets which over the years have sustained extensive dust and scratches in storage. The images have been cleaned up to reduce the damage without interfering too much with the original photographic quality.

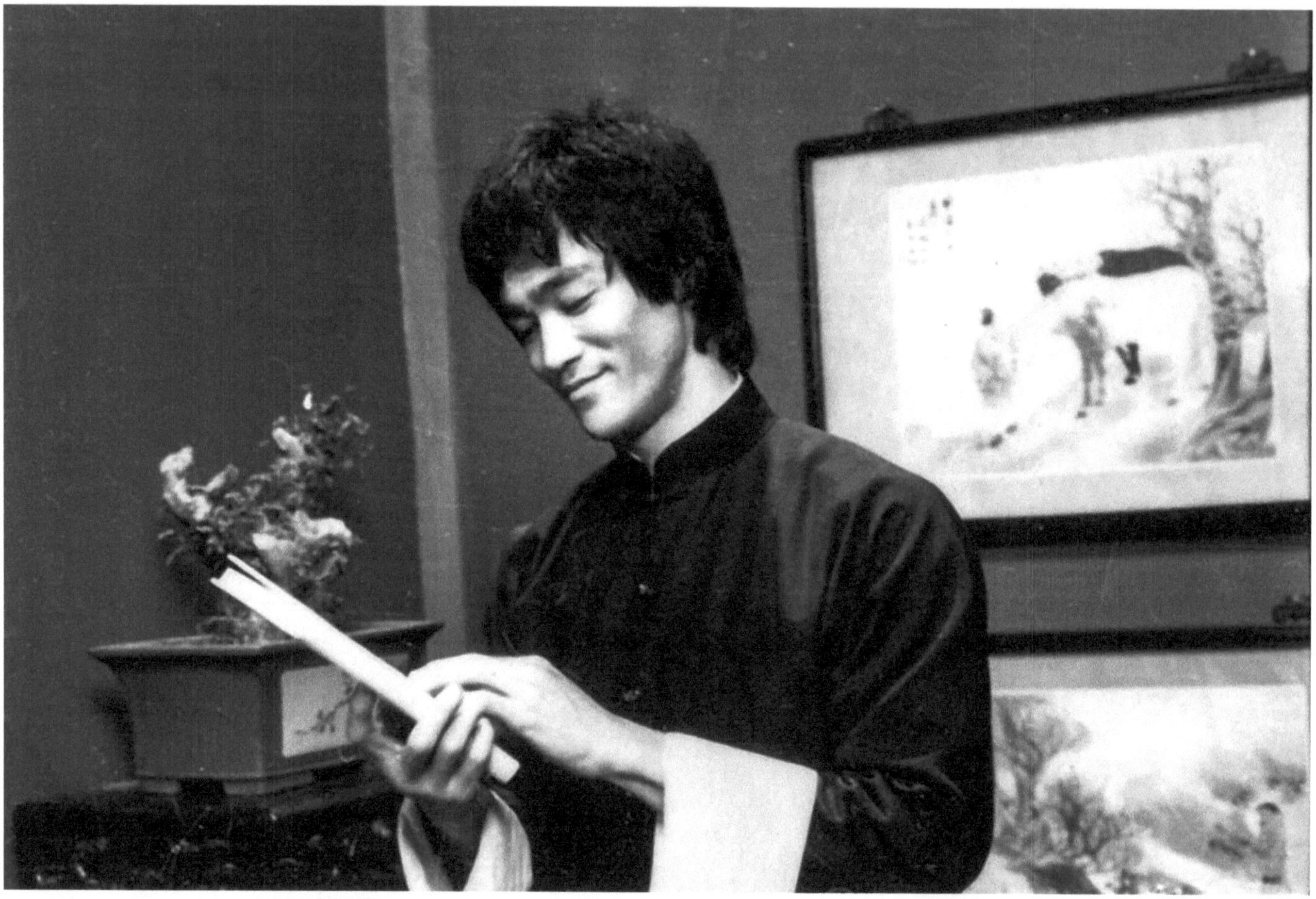

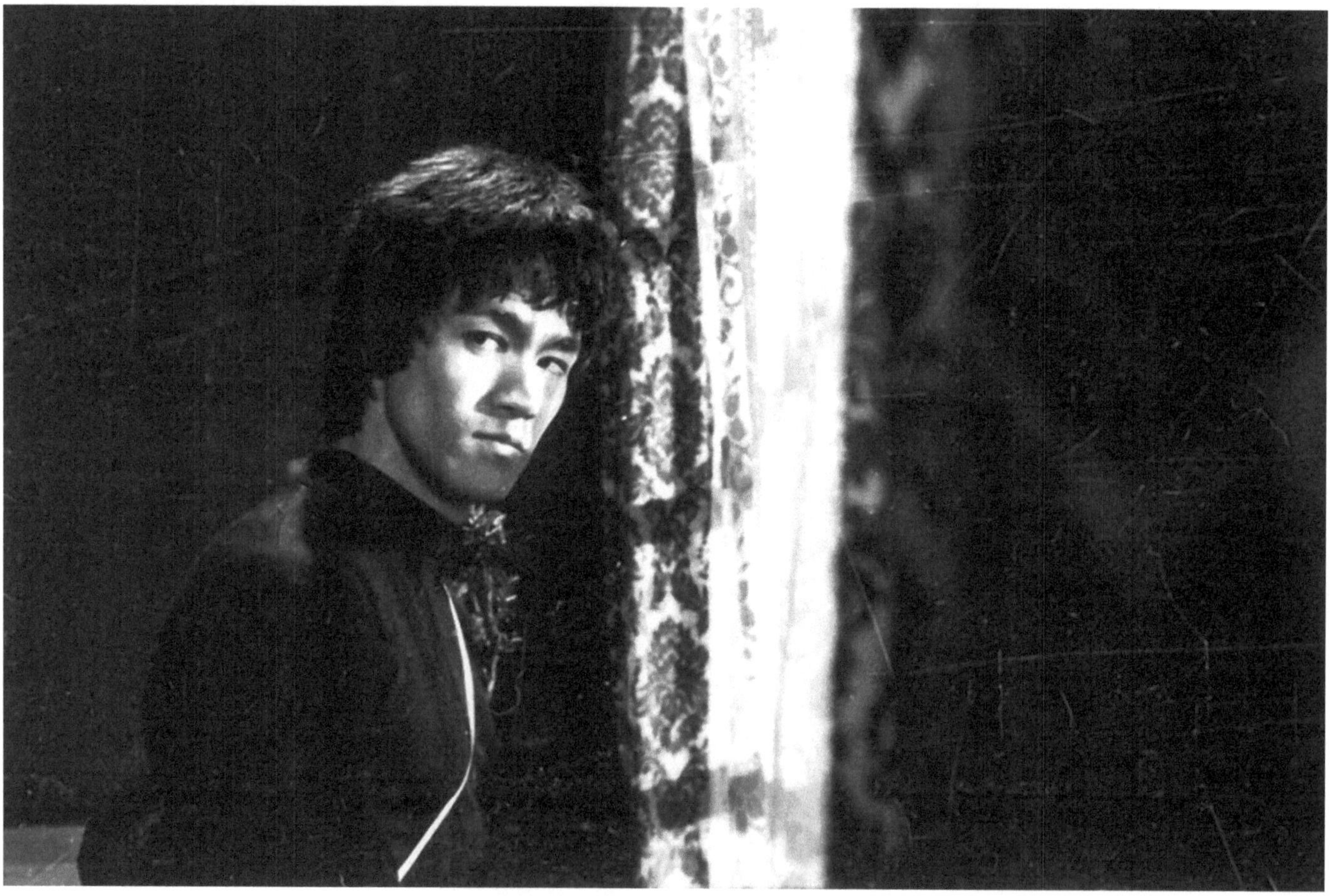

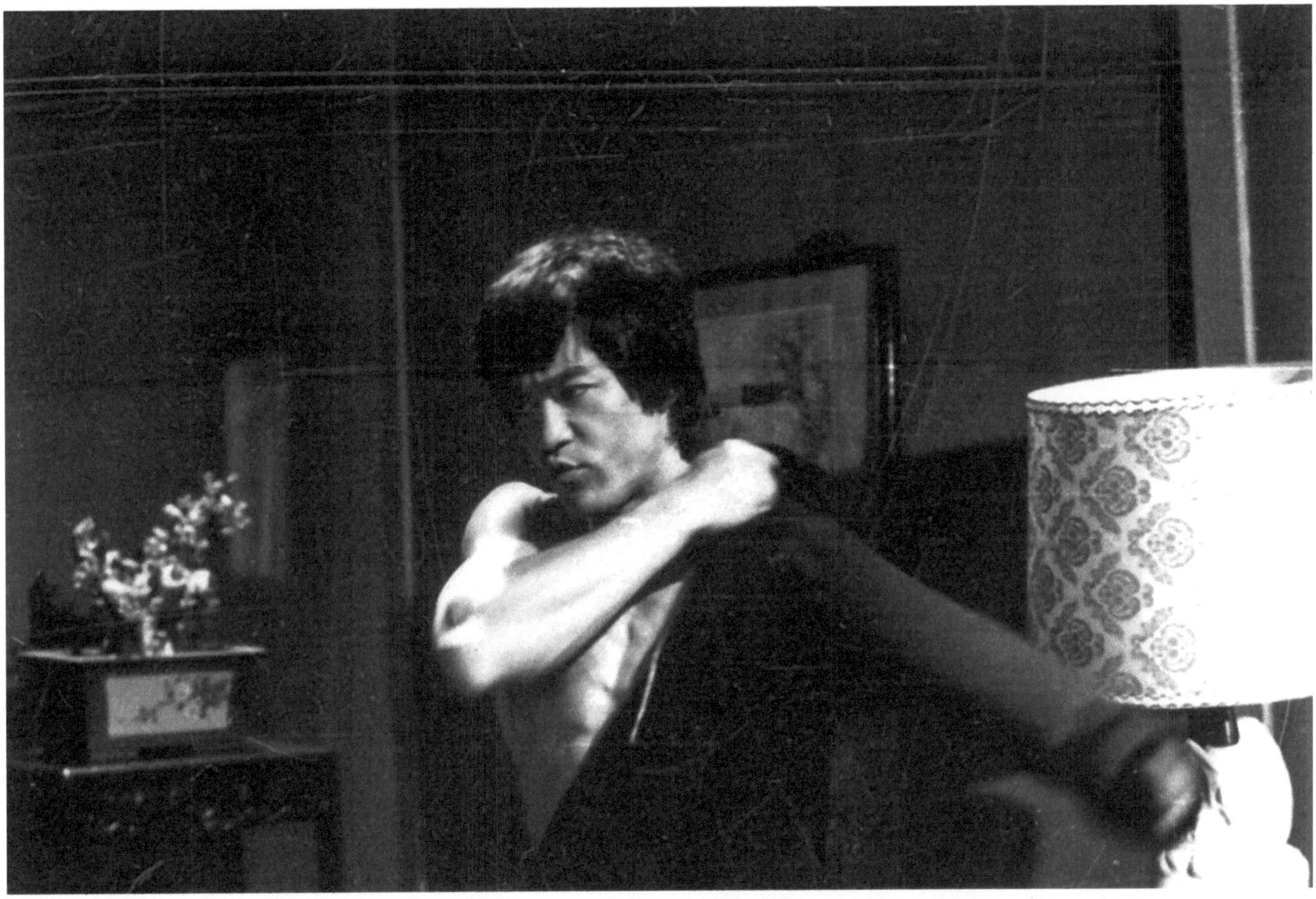

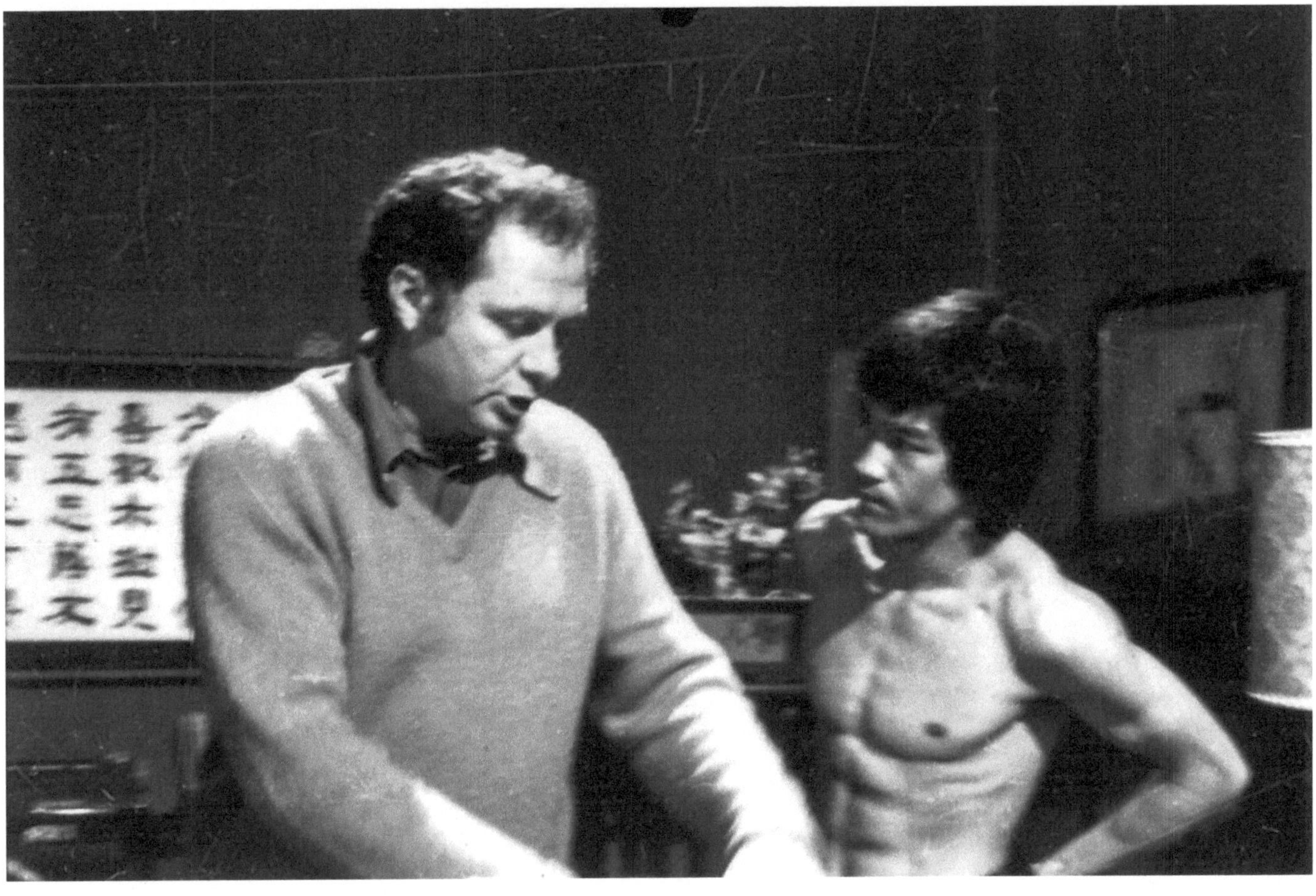

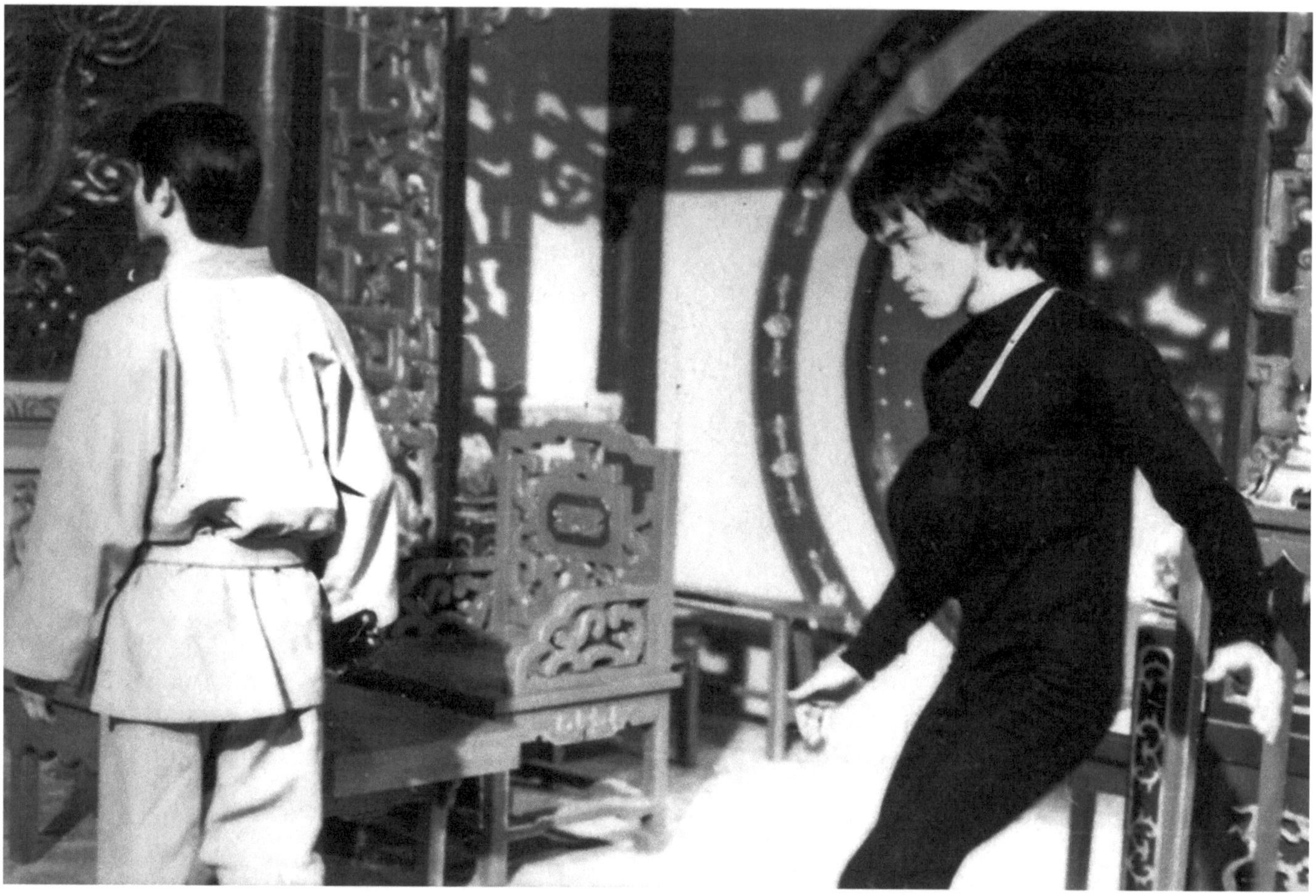

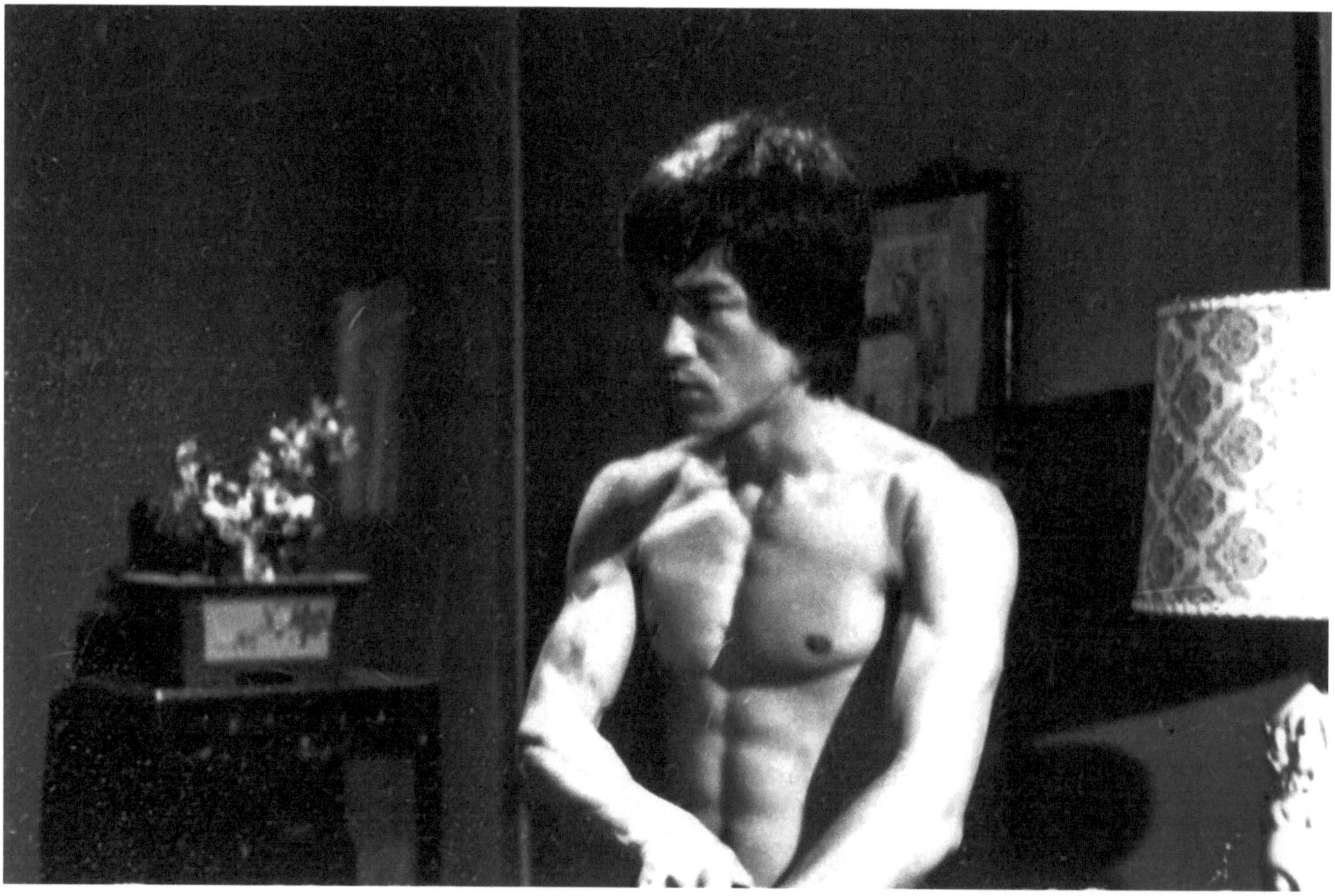

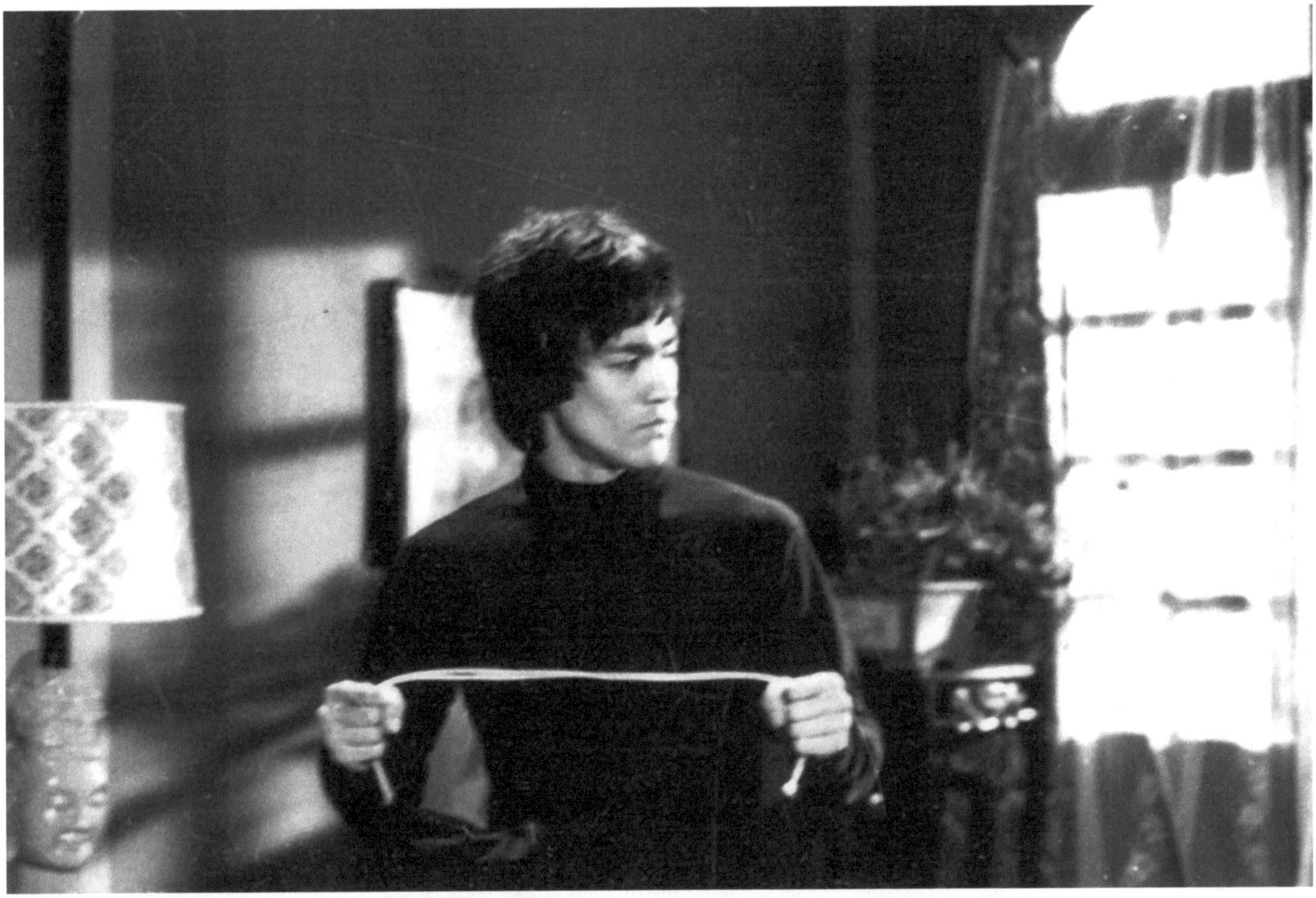

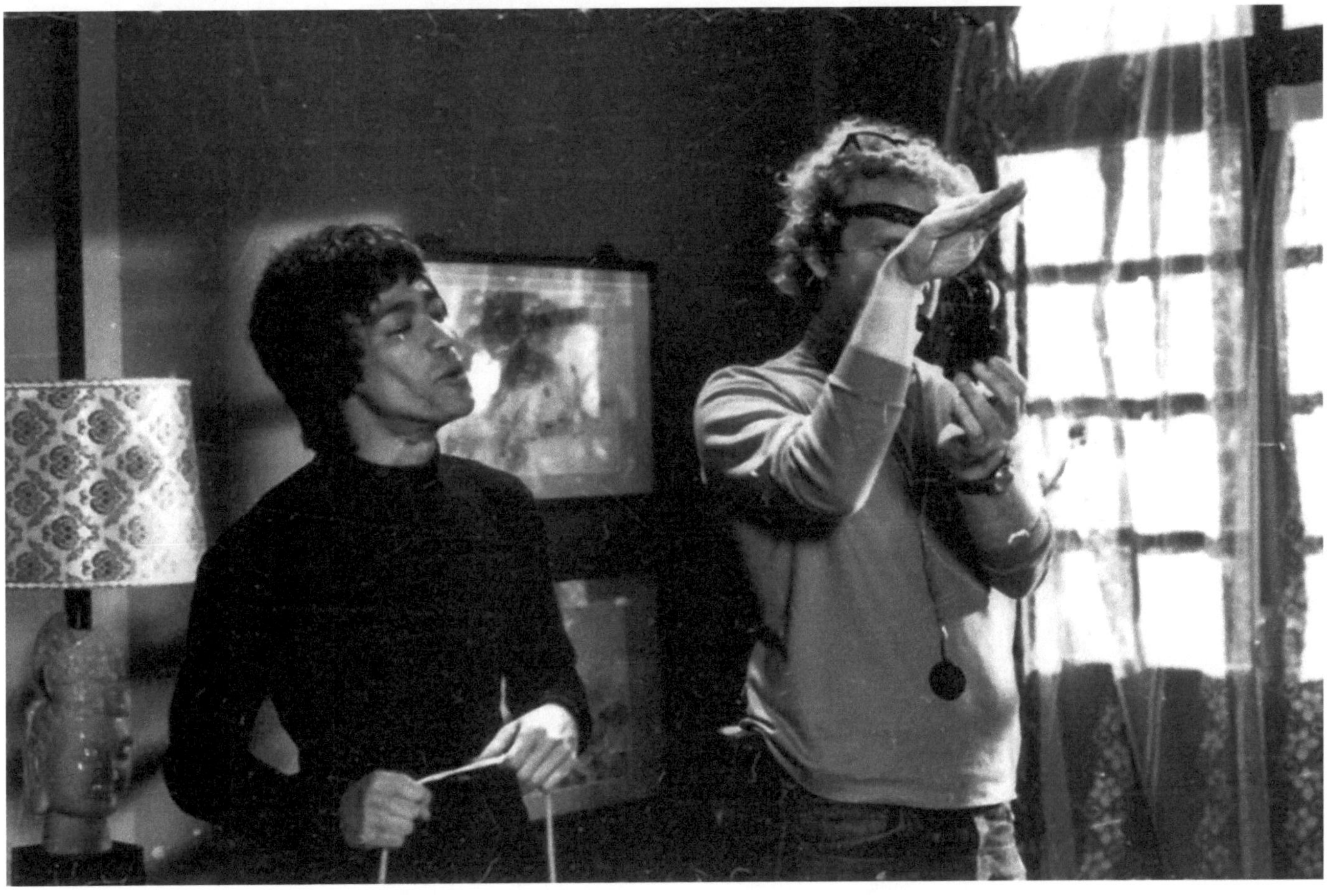

# THE STAFF IS AN EXTENSION OF THE FIST

Enter the Dragon Photographic Collection – Vol. 2

# BATTLE ON THE WALL

**The action** moves from the battlefield to a narrow ledge, changing the landscape of the action as Lee goes in hot pursuit of Han, sending an unlucky guard sprawling to the ground.

*Enter the Dragon* Photographic Collection – Vol. 2

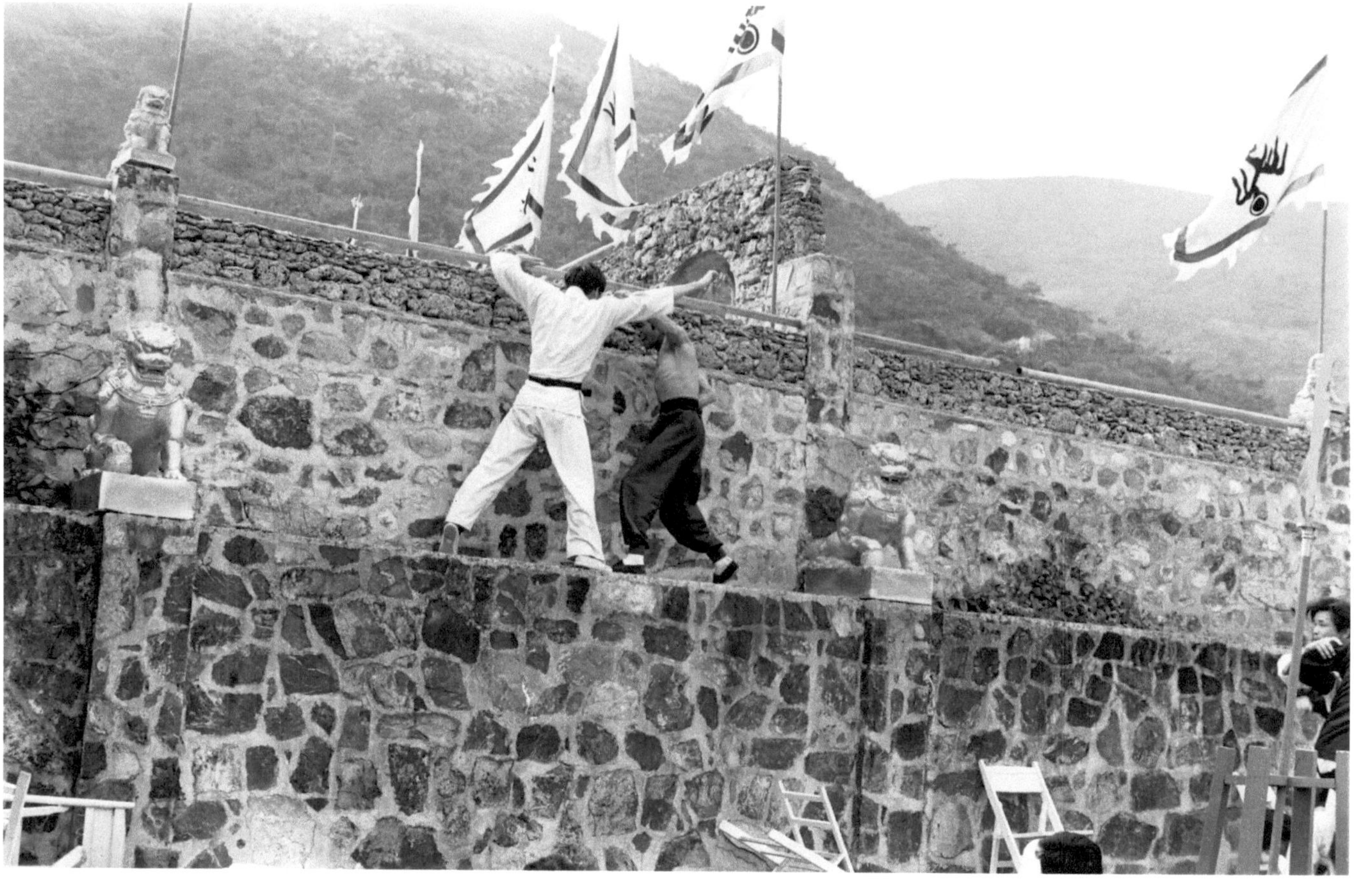

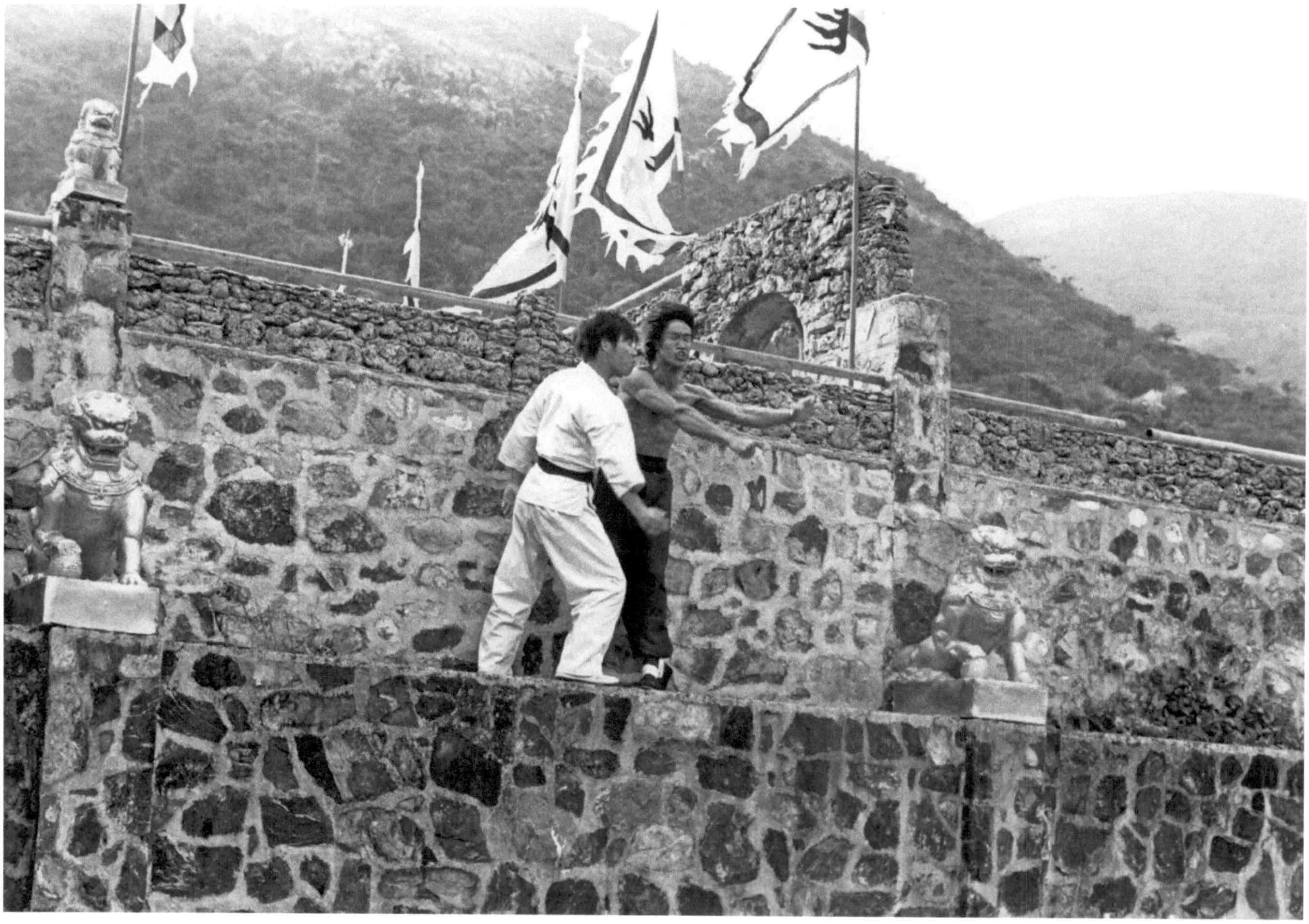

Enter the Dragon Photographic Collection – Vol. 2

# THE FINAL BATTLE

Enter the Dragon Photographic Collection – Vol. 2

*Enter the Dragon* Photographic Collection – Vol. 2

82  *Enter the Dragon* Photographic Collection – Vol. 2

Enter the Dragon Photographic Collection – Vol. 2

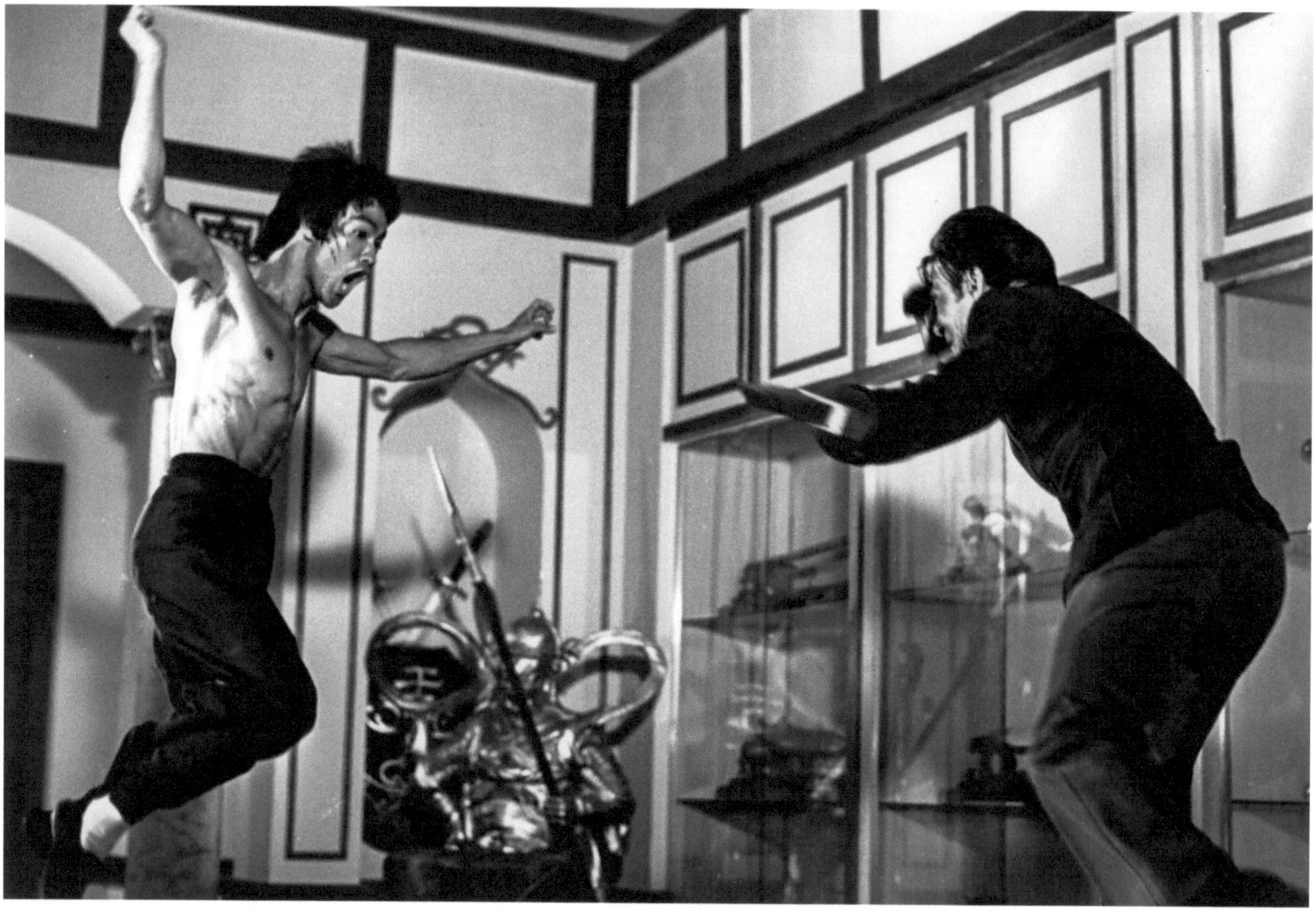

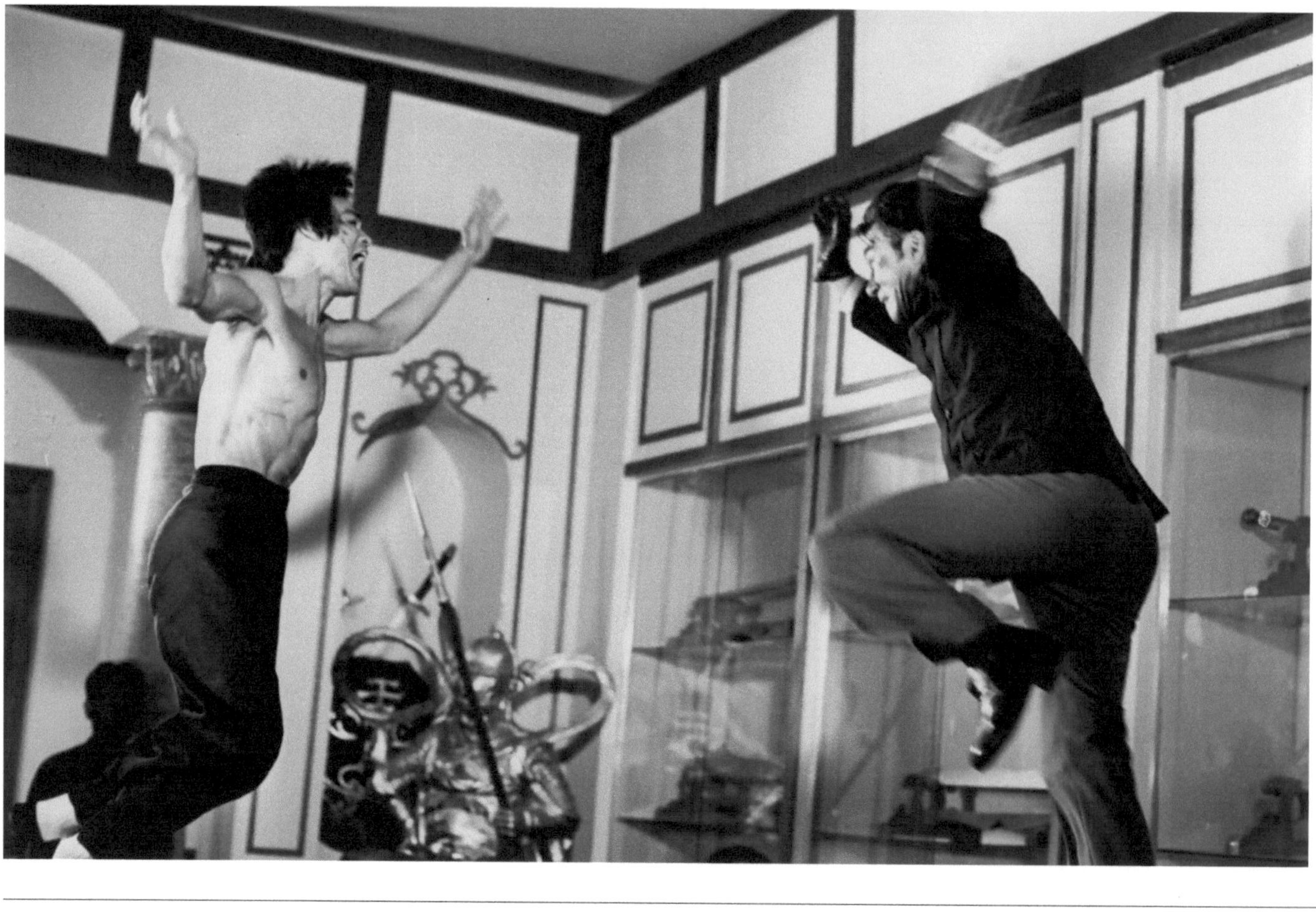

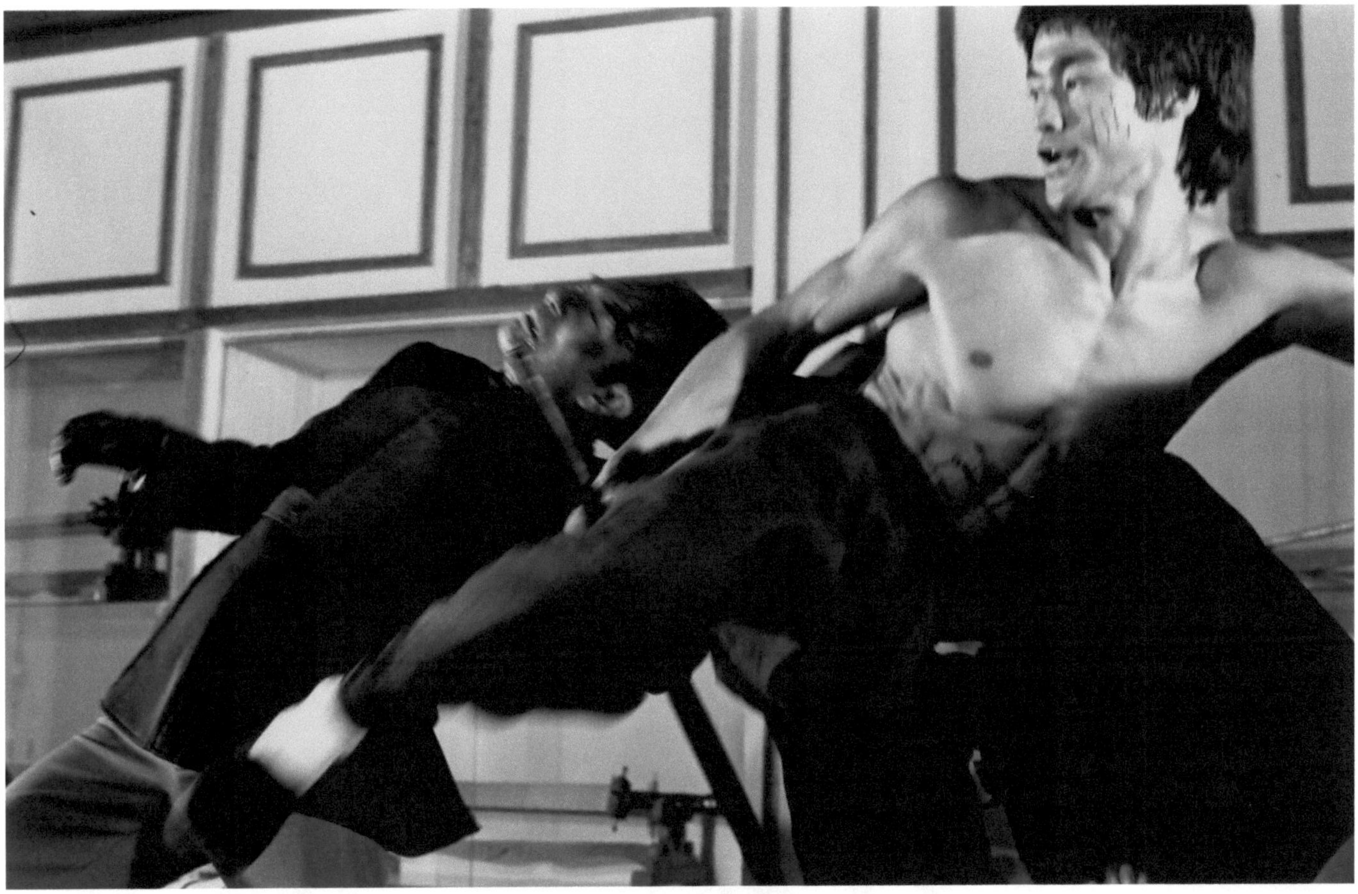

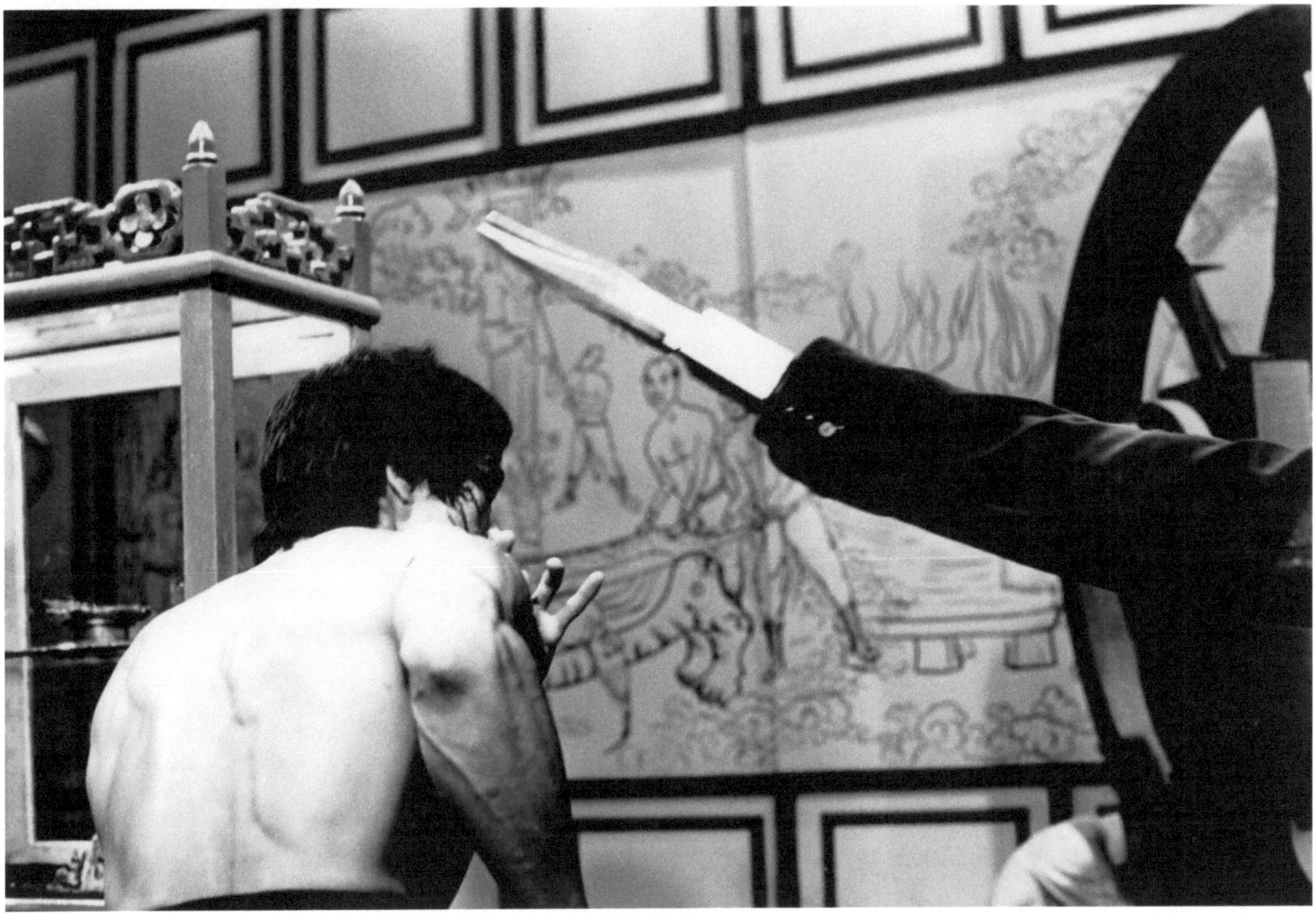

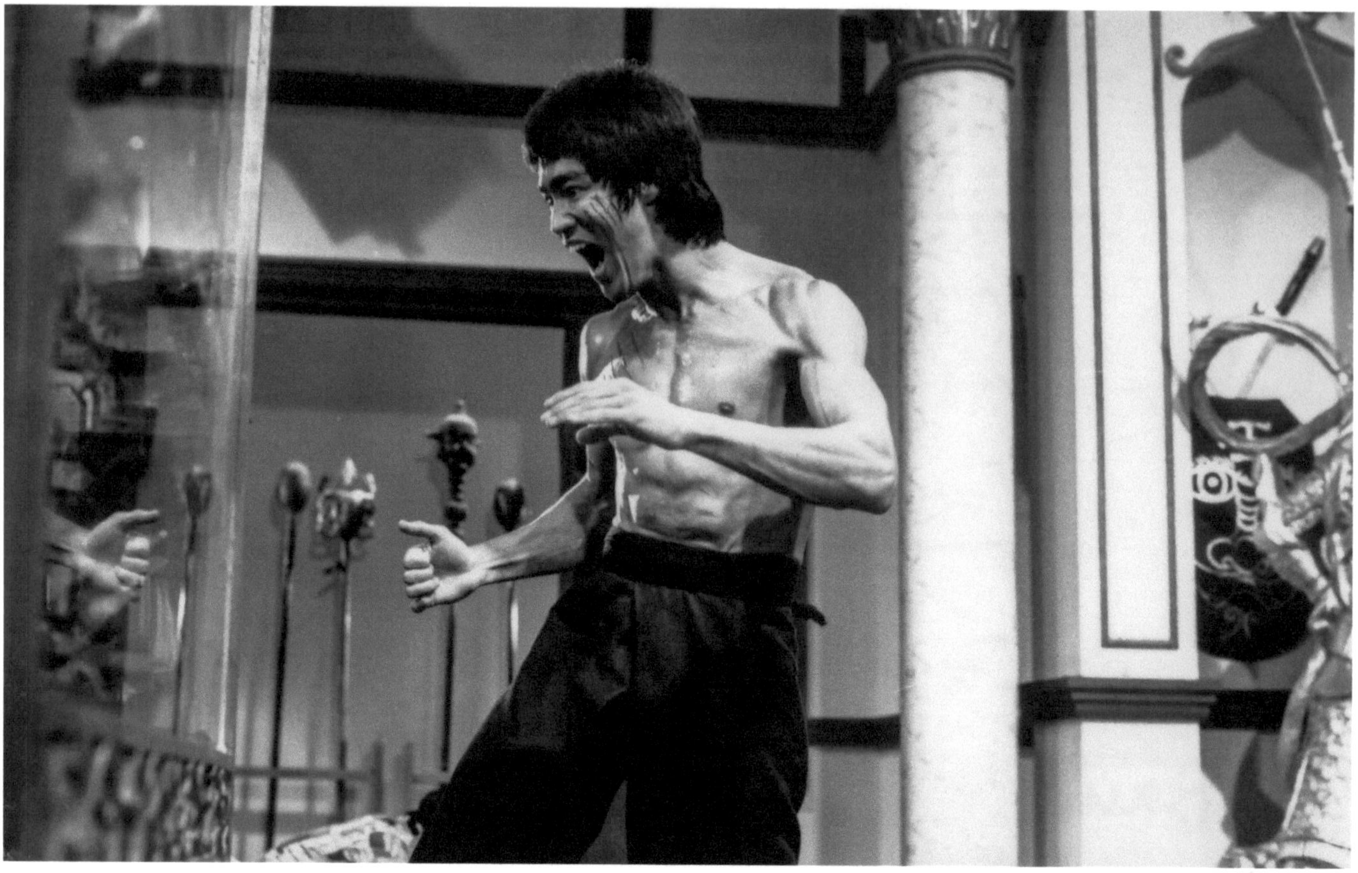

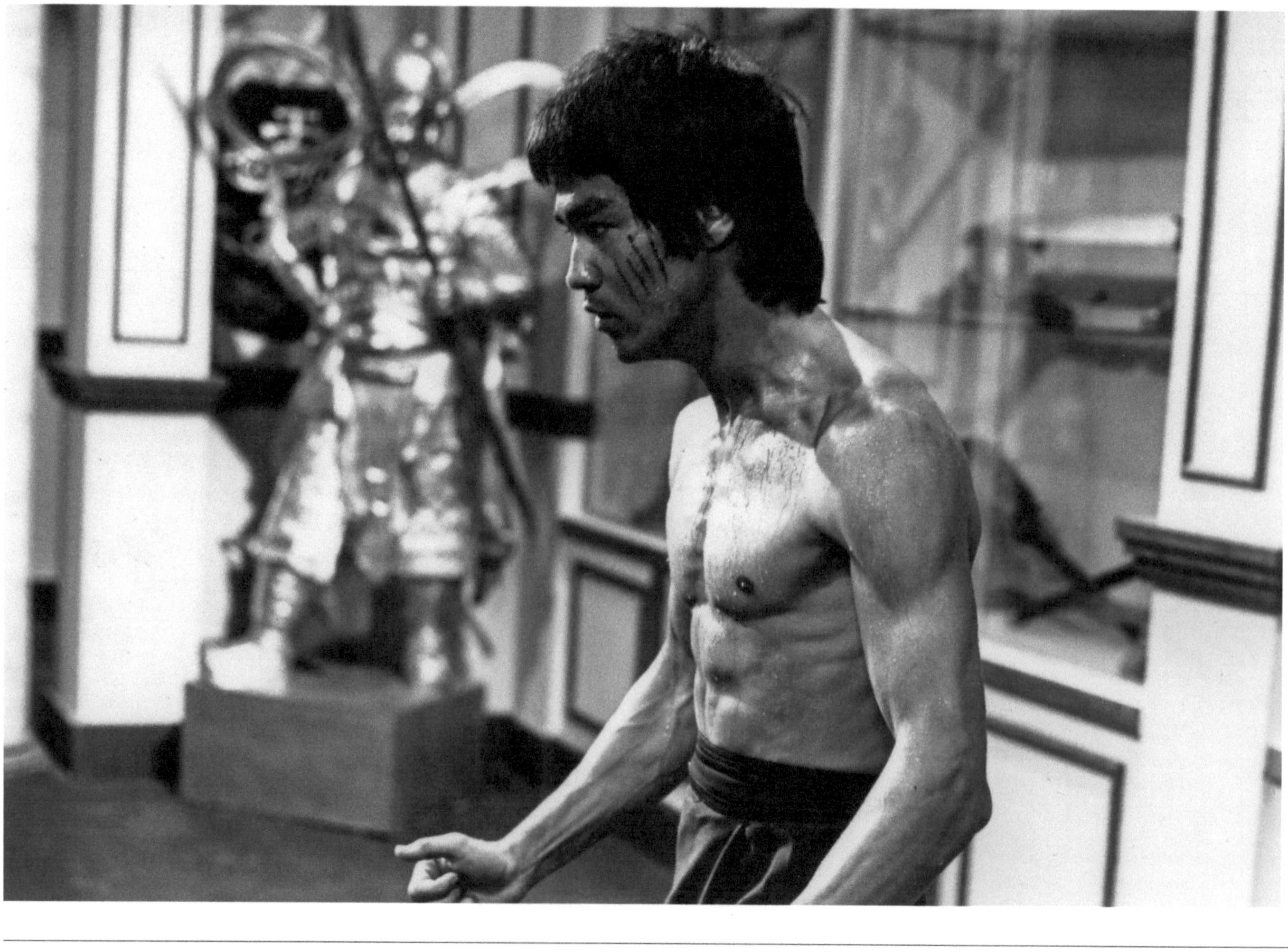

One of the most memorable fights as Bruce finally faces Han before the final confrontation in the room of mirrors. Yuen Wah once again doubles, this time for Han for the more trickier fight sequences.

# CONTACT SHEETS

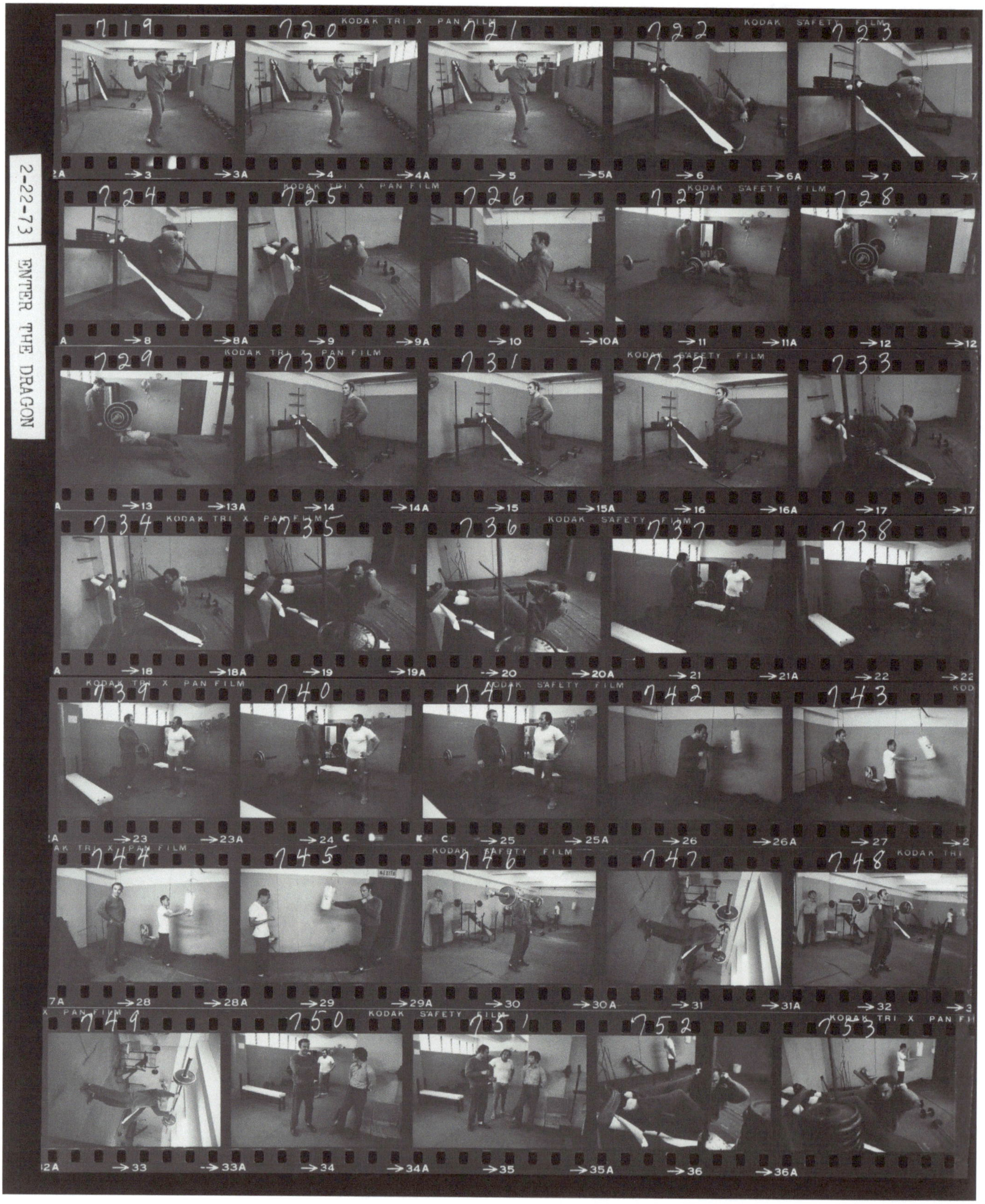

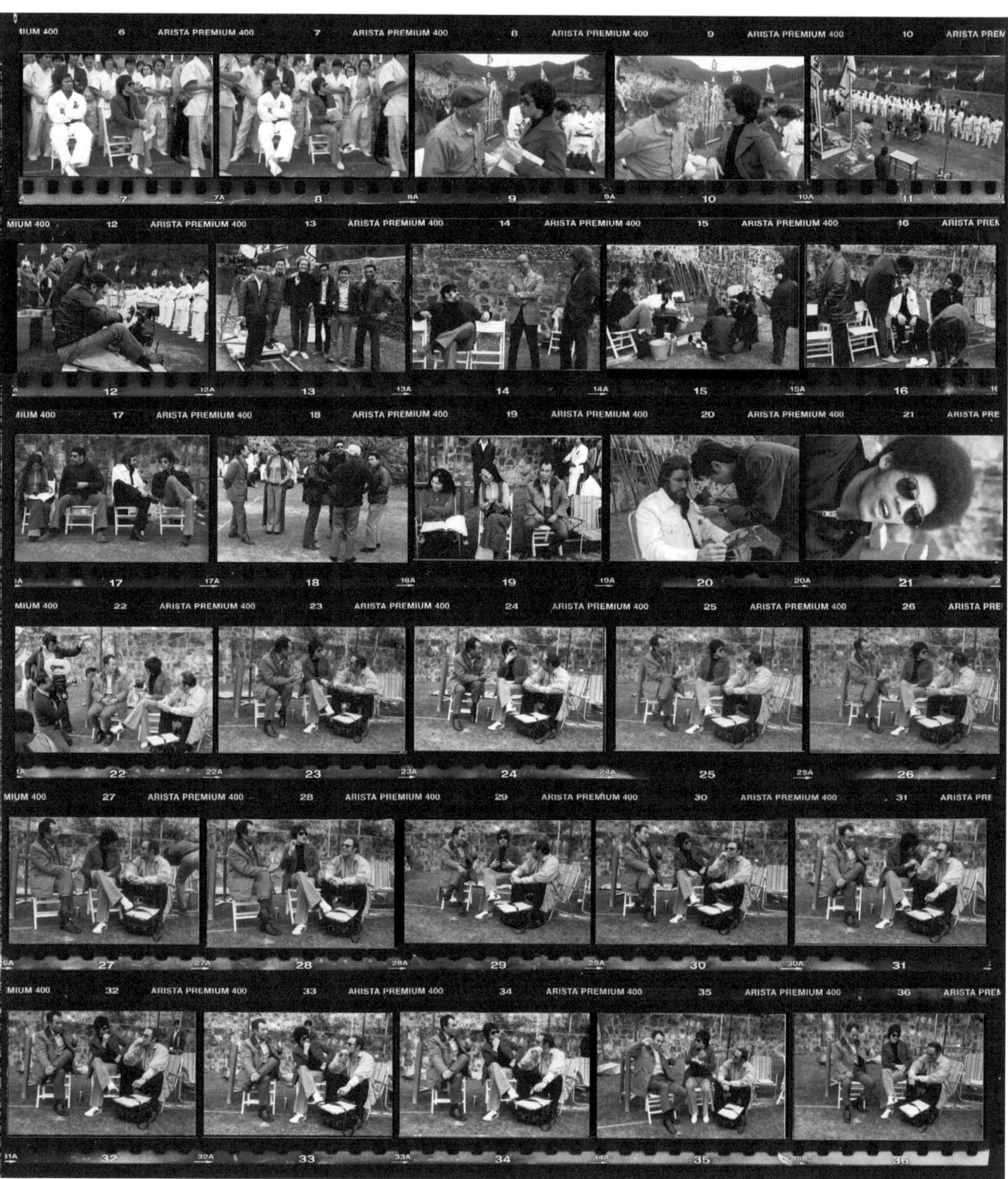

Enter the Dragon Photographic Collection – Vol. 2

Enter the Dragon Photographic Collection – Vol. 2

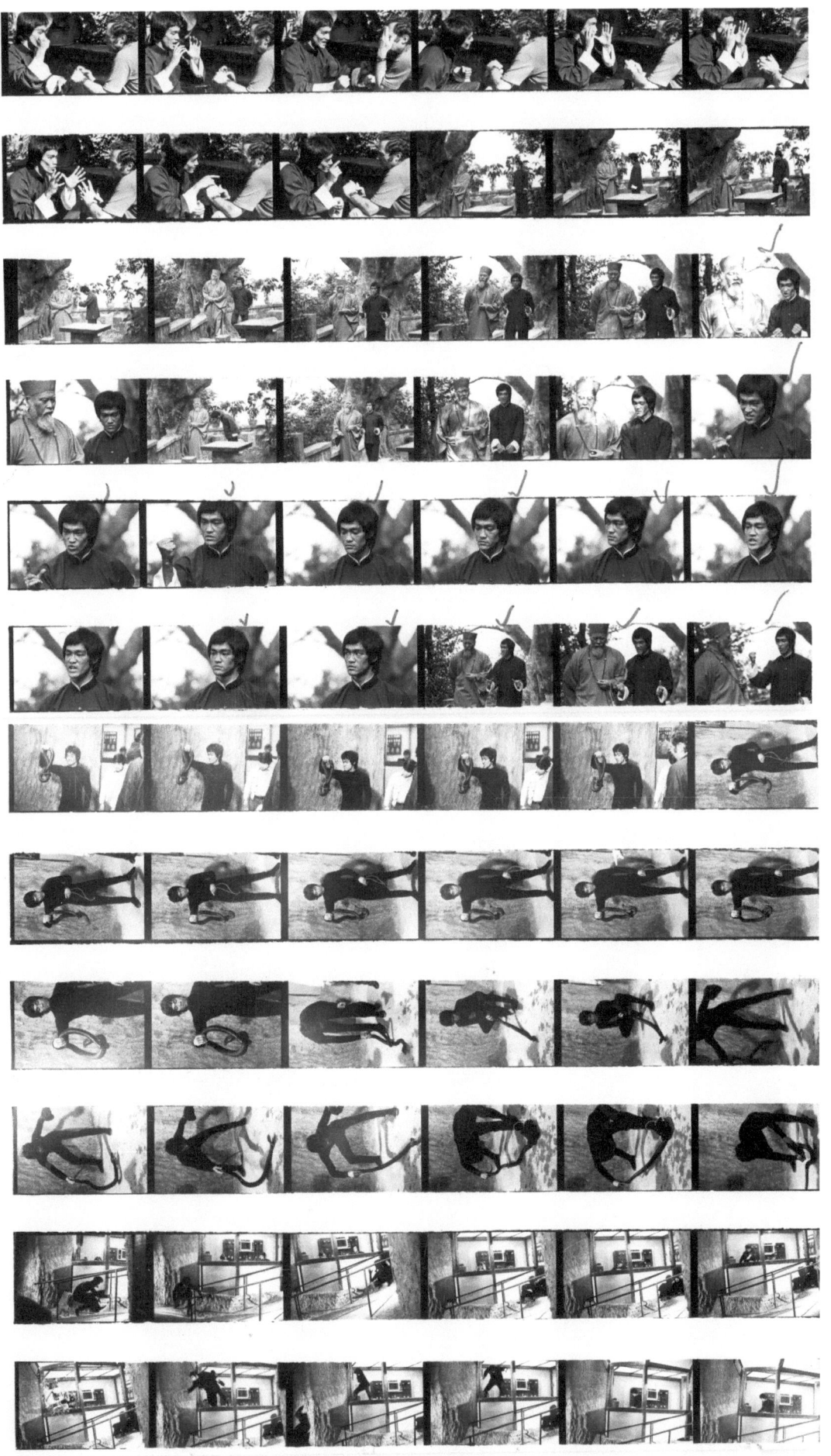

Enter the Dragon Photographic Collection – Vol. 2

www.ingramcontent.com/pod-product-compliance
Lightning Source LLC
Chambersburg PA
CBHW041506220426
43661CB00016B/1263